The George Bernard Shaw Vegetarian Cook Book

First American Appearance through
the courtesy of JULIAN BACH
Settings by TONY MATTHEWS
Scenic Design by FRANK R. SLOAN
Production Supervised by MOLLIE M. TORRAS
Special Arrangements for the Original Production by
BOBS PINKERTON, ALAN HARVEY & DODIE GERSON

New Revised Edition by
DOROTHY R. BATES
1987
Cover Art by PETER HOYT
Production Supervised by LOUISE HAGLER

The Book Publishing Company

presents

The George Bernard Shaw Vegetarian Cook Book

in six acts

based on George Bernard Shaw's favorite recipes

book by **Alice Laden**

(former cook/housekeeper to G.B.S.)

Original Edition edited and adapted by **R.J. Minney**

Revised New Edition by **Dorothy R. Bates**

STARRING

Walnut Soufflé   Vegetable Charlotte

and featuring

SAVORY EGGPLANT   RISOTTO   TOMATOES BENGAL

CUMBERLAND SAUCE

cheese twists   *leek soup*   *nut-rice roast*   *spicy sauce*

QUEEN OF PUDDINGS and TRIFLE

New Production Directed by
THE BOOK PUBLISHING COMPANY
Summertown, TN

Revised New Edition
Pubished by:
THE BOOK PUBLISHING COMPANY
Summertown, TN 38483

First Published in the United States in 1973 by
TAPLINGER PUBLISHING CO. INC. New York, New York

Library of Congress Card Catalog Number 86-73060

ISBN 0-913990-51-5

The Cast *(in order of appearance)*

THE PLOT THICKENS... *sauces*

GRAND FINALES... *desserts*

The George Bernard Shaw Vegetarian Cook Book

Prologue... *an introduction*

For the first quarter of a century of his life George Bernard Shaw ate meat. It was not until he was twenty-five that he became a vegetarian.

What prompted the change? Shaw said it was the poet Shelley "who opened my eyes to the savagery of my diet." He quoted two lines from Shelley's *The Revolt of Islam:*

> "Never again may blood of bird or beast
> Stain with its venomous stream a human feast!"

But it is quite probable that poverty provided the initial stimulus. For some years after he came to London Shaw was without work, nor did he want a job. He had decided that he was a genius and he was going to prove it as a writer. In the meantime he was entirely dependent on his mother, who had left her husband and now earned her living by giving singing lessons. She allowed him to occupy a small room in her house in Kensington and gave him a little pocket money. This he used to pay his tram fare to the British Museum, where he spent hours each day in the library, and to buy his midday meal. Often he walked, to save the fares, but even so he couldn't afford to spend much on lunch. After a time he discovered that there were small restaurants in side streets which served only vegetarian dishes and these were within his means.

He spent five years writing novels, each of which was flung back at him by publishers. He also did some hack writing which brought him no more than £5 or so a year. So he was still dependent on the very small allowance he received from his mother, and thus his visits to the vegetarian restaurants continued.

Then in 1881 Shaw gave up eating meat altogether. He informed his mother of this, but she did not concern herself much with what her son did. She was too busy earning a living for both of them and simply instructed the housemaid to prepare such food for him as he wanted. Thereafter, in the mornings the maid took a bowl of oatmeal porridge up to his room and placed it on his desk beside his shabby old typewriter. He would dip his spoon into the bowl from time to time and leave it unfinished amid his sheaves of typed pages. Often it was there for days, the porridge cold and gluey, for the maid was not allowed to touch anything on his desk in case she disturbed the various heaped piles of his papers. But whatever the initial stimulus, Shaw maintained his vegetarianism on both ethical and health grounds. "Meat is poison to the system," he said. "No one should live on dead things." And again, "Animals are our fellow creatures. I feel a strong sense of kinship with them." And further, "It is beneficial to one's health not to be carnivorous. The strongest animals, such as the bull, are vegetarians. Look at me. I have ten times as much good health and energy as a meat-eater." He was certainly extremely healthy, always fit, energetic both mentally and physically, and lived to be within sight of his ninety-fifth birthday. He once revealed his vision of the happy scene at his funeral: "My hearse will be followed not by mourning coaches but by herds of oxen, sheep, swine, flocks of poultry and a small travelling aquarium of live fish, all wearing white scarves in honour of the man who perished rather than eat his fellow creatures."

Shaw not only refused to eat flesh but also did not want meat fat, meat bouillon cubes, or meat essences to be used in the cooking of his meals and, being a teetotaler, he would not allow alcohol in any form to be incorporated in any dish.

His mother, who was the provider of his specialized meals during the seventeen years he continued to live with her as a vegetarian, did not, as I have mentioned, involve herself at all with what went on in the kitchen. Shaw ate such vegetables as were prepared to go with the meat courses served to the others, and he

"My hearse will be followed not by mourning coaches but by herds of oxen, sheep, swine, flocks of poultry and a small traveling aquarium of live fish, all wearing white scarves in honour of the man who perished rather than eat his fellow creature."

had to use his powers of persuasion with the cook to prevent her from using meat fat in their preparation.

In 1898, when he was forty-two, he married Charlotte Payne-Townshend, and the position became very different. Though the new Mrs. Shaw was not a vegetarian she was an admirable organizer and she personally supervised all his meals. The Shaws entertained constantly. The guests were usually meat-eaters and G.B.S.'s meals, which were prepared separately, would be served by one maid while another maid served Mrs. Shaw and their guests. There were cocktails in the drawing room beforehand and red and white wines at the table, while the teetotal host sipped his glass of water.

Shaw's meals during his forty-five years of marriage were varied and appetizing, as they had never been at his mother's house. His wife's menus for him included vegetable pies, nut cutlets, cauliflower au gratin, cheese flans, vegetable curries, raw vegetables and fruit. Shaw had a weakness for highly sweetened desserts and for ices and sundaes, and all these were provided as a result of his wife's devoted attention. After her death in 1943 someone had to be found to take over.

During her last, long illness Mrs. Shaw had been nursed by Mrs. Alice Laden, a young widow from Aberdeen, and after his wife's death Shaw managed to persuade Mrs. Laden to stay on as his housekeeper. Shaw was then eighty-seven and intending to spend the rest of his life at his house in the country at Ayot St. Lawrence. At first Mrs. Laden, who had stayed there from time to time during the eight months she had been nursing Mrs. Shaw, told Shaw that she had no wish to live there. It was a small, quiet village. There were no diversions, not even a cinema, and the nearest town, Welwyn, was five miles away and there were no trains or buses to get her there. But at last, touched by his loneliness, she agreed to go.

It was his good fortune that she was well-equipped to take charge of his vegetarian meals, for her husband had been a strict vegetarian and she had undertaken, before her marriage, an extended course of training in vegetarian cookery at the Domestic Science Training Guild in Aberdeen under the famous German cookery expert, Mrs. Gompertz. The training took several months, and eventually each pupil had to prepare an eight or ten-course vegetarian dinner for a large party of guests. "Mrs. Gompertz was an excellent teacher," Mrs. Laden has told me. "Very painstaking with her pupils, and if my pastries are praised as being light and tasty I owe my skill to her. Incidentally, Mr. Shaw didn't care much for pastry."

It was in 1943 that Mrs. Laden first took on the job of cook-housekeeper and moved down to Ayot St. Lawrence. At that time food was being severely rationed. Only necessities were being imported, but the ingredients of a vegetarian diet range beyond ordinary necessities, and regularly she was forced to set out on a difficult search, from shop to shop and from town to town. Because he didn't want to put on any weight, Shaw was very insistent that the calories should be carefully worked out for each meal. This is what Mrs. Laden has to say on this touchy subject:

Mr. Shaw was very particular about the calories in his food. These had to be most carefully worked out. The calories in each dish had to be weighed and the total for the meal had to be right. The reason for this was his concern not to put on any weight. He was, as you know, a very tall man--over six foot in height--with a fine, slender figure, and this he was resolved to retain. He stood on the scales every morning to make sure that there was not a fraction of an ounce of difference in his weight from one day to the next. He retained his figure to the end. His health was perfect. He never suffered from indigestion.

What was more, Shaw told Mrs. Laden that she should buy only the best, that his meals must be varied, and, finally, that she was not to touch black market goods, none of which made the search any easier. Imported vegetables and fruits such as eggplants, oranges, pineapples, and bananas were unobtainable through any other channels. Shaw had to put his chauffeur-driven Rolls-Royce at Mrs. Laden's disposal for the quest, and quite often she had to go as far as London, twenty-five miles away, to find what was required by the great man.

He constantly complained about the cost. "I'm a poor man," he used to say. But he never denied himself anything. Alice Laden remembers the following incident:

He asked me once if I had enough money to pay the bills. 'Yes,' I said. 'I change your checks at the butcher's.' He exploded. 'What?' he gasped. 'At the butcher's? You know I don't eat meat. I don't want the butcher to handle any of my checks.' I explained that his checks had always been cashed at the butcher's—even in Mrs. Shaw's time. 'You must stop that,' he said. 'I shall open an account for you at the bank. You must cash them there in future.' I was glad of that because the butcher was not always able to cash £50 check.

Even after the war was ended, Shaw's food remained very expensive, in contrast to his earlier days when vegetarian restaurants had saved him money, because he insisted on having the very best butter and cream, varieties of excellent cheese, and a large assortment of the finest nuts. Food had become very important to him and a great deal of time was spent over meals. Shaw's breakfast occupied two and a half hours of the morning, and lunch two and a half hours of the afternoon. Dinner, a relatively light meal, was over in an hour and a quarter.

Afternoon tea, so much favored by the British, was observed by him but he did not drink tea. He had a large glass of milk to wash down the numerous chocolate biscuits and slices of fruit cake he enjoyed so much. Mrs. Laden often found him in the evenings seated with a bowl of sugar in his lap stuffing it into his mouth by the spoonful. Sometimes it was a jar of honey instead.

"I don't know how it is he didn't get sick, popping so many spoonfuls of honey into his tummy. I knew he was very fond of sweet things. I always used honey instead of sugar when I made his dessert. I even put some honey or sugar into his soup. With his dish of raw vegetables he always had sweet chutney. And I rarely saw him—between meals mind you—without a large chunk of cake heavily coated with sugar icing in his hand. One day, as he walked into the street to say goodbye to Greer Garson, who always came to see him when she was over from Hollywood, I saw him munching at the same time on an enormous piece of cake covered with marzipan and thick icing."

One had to get used to the sight of this talented, highly intellectual old man eating sweets like a schoolboy. Fortunately, a normal vegetarian meal is far more digestible than meat, and Shaw remained extremely healthy throughout his life.

"Not a single day was spent in bed by him," Mrs. Laden told me, "until he fell in the garden a few weeks before his death at the wonderful age of ninety-four. Occasionally, in the last year or two, he was a little off-color, but it soon passed. After dozing for an hour or two in a chair he got up and was as brisk and as lively as ever. I mentioned this to the doctor and was told that if I gave him a dram of whiskey when he felt off-color, it would help. I had to do this furtively of course. Mr. Shaw would have been horrified if he knew, so I had to disguise it as best I could and I did so by putting it in his soup so that he shouldn't detect it. But I think he did suspect, for a few days before he died he said to me, after finishing some soup, 'You have been playing tricks on me, Mrs. Laden.' "

The recipes Mrs. Laden devised for Shaw are set out in the following pages. Although even Shaw himself was never allowed into her kitchen to discuss his meals, his hearty appetite and continuing good health were signs of his majestic approval. (The only exception Mrs. Laden made to this rule was for President Nehru who, when he arrived with a basket of mangoes as a present for Shaw, was actually invited in to advise on their preparation.)

R.J. Minney

a word about these recipes...

George Bernard Shaw was a vegetarian long before facts about good nutrition were widely known. Proof that he ate well-balanced meals was his vigorous physical and intellectual health into his 95th year. And despite his love of sweets and rich desserts, this paragon of the arts remained slim all his life.

As soy foods were not widely available, his sources of protein were nuts, legumes, cheese and eggs. Vitamins and minerals were amply supplied by fruits, vegetables and grains. In winter, the most available vegetables were potatoes, onion and cabbage and his cook used these in imaginative ways.

These recipes follow his food preferences, using brown rice instead of white, honey rather that sugar except in some dessert recipes. Seasoning is a matter of personal taste, you may wish to substitute sage or marjoram for thyme or several herbs in place of salt.

I share George Bernard Shaw's sentiment when he said, "There is no love sincerer than the love of good food."

Dorothy R. Bates

The Curtain Rises... *appetizers*

Cheese Olive Balls

1 7-ounce jar medium size stuffed olives
½ pound cheddar cheese, grated
½ cup butter
1½ cups flour
¼ teaspoon salt
1 teaspoon paprika
dash of cayenne

Drain olives, dry on paper towels. Mix cheese, butter, flour and seasonings. Take a small piece of dough, press flat between thumb and palm of hand, roll it around an olive. Press edges of dough to seal. Place balls on ungreased baking sheet. These can be frozen and defrosted to bake later. Bake at 400° about 15 minutes and serve hot.

Yield: 60 balls

Olive Stuffed Eggs

4 eggs, hard cooked
2 tablespoons mayonnaise (page 54)
1 teaspoon prepared mustard
½ teaspoon salt
8 stuffed olives, chopped
dash of pepper

Cut eggs in half lengthwise, remove yolks. Mash yolks with a fork, adding other ingredients. Fill egg white shells.

Yield: 8 stuffed eggs

Chutney Cheese Squares

2 slices whole wheat toast
2 tablespoons chutney
2 ounces cheese, grated

Cut each slice of toast into 4 squares. Put a scant teaspoon of chutney on each, top with cheese. Bake at 450° about 4 minutes.

Yield: 8 squares

Onion Cheese Puffs

2 slices whole wheat bread
2 tablespoons chopped green onion
2 tablespoons grated cheese
2 tablespoons mayonnaise
paprika

Trim crusts from bread, cut each slice into 4 triangles. Mix onion and cheese with mayonnaise. Spread on bread. Sprinkle with paprika. Bake at 450° for 5 minutes.

Yield: 8 Puffs

Cucumber Canapes

6 slices whole wheat bread
1 medium cucumber, thinly sliced
1 teaspoon salt
a few onion slices
⅓ cup sour cream
1 teaspoon dill weed.

Cut each slice of bread into 2 rounds with cookie cutter. Sprinkle cucumber and onion slices with salt and chill for 30 minutes. Press out excess liquid, mix slices with sour cream. Arrange on bread rounds and sprinkle with dill weed.

Yield: 12 rounds

Cheese Twists

¼ cup cold butter
½ cup small-curd cottage cheese
⅔ cup flour
⅓ cup parmesan cheese

Put flour, cottage cheese and parmesan into processor. Slice in the cold butter. Process a few seconds, shape into ball of dough. On lightly floured board, pat into oblong and roll out to about 16″ by 6″. Cut into strips 6″long and ¾″ wide, twist each strip. Place on ungreased baking sheet. Bake at 425° 7 to 8 minutes. Sprinkle with additional parmesan and serve warm. If made ahead, reheat in moderate oven before serving.

Yield: 24 twists

Stuffed Mushrooms

12 large mushrooms
2 tablespoons butter
1 shallot, finely chopped
⅓ cup milk
⅓ cup fine bread crumbs
1 egg, lightly beaten
1 tablespoon minced parsley
¼ teaspoon each of salt, pepper and thyme

Remove stems of mushrooms and chop stems. Place caps rounded side down in 1 tablespoon melted butter and sauté until lightly browned. Remove caps to baking dish. Melt the other tablespoon of butter and sauté chopped stems and the shallots until softened. Mix milk, egg, crumbs, stems, parsley and seasonings. Fill caps. Bake at 425° about 10 minutes. Serve hot.

12 stuffed caps

Tomatoes Bengal

4 slices bread
vegetable oil
2 large tomatoes
curry powder
salt and pepper
½ cup chutney, chopped

Cut crusts off bread, rounding corners. Sauté bread in a small amount of hot vegetable oil to crisp. Drain on paper towels and keep warm. Peel tomatoes and cut 4 thick slices. Spread bread rounds with chutney, top with tomato slice, sprinkle with salt, pepper and a pinch of curry powder. Bake at 350° 6-8 minutes and serve hot.

4 appetizers

Armenian Beans

1 cup dried white lima beans
3 cups water
1 teaspoon salt
1 carrot, thinly sliced
1 stalk celery, thinly sliced
1 clove garlic, minced
2 tablespoons olive oil
2 tablespoons parsley, finely chopped
1 teaspoon dill weed
¼ teaspoon black pepper

Rinse the beans, place in saucepan, pour the 3 cups of boiling water over the beans. Boil, covered, for 2 minutes. Let stand one hour, then simmer for about 1½ hours until tender, covered. Add salt when beans are nearly cooked. Heat small skillet, add olive oil and lightly sauté the carrots, celery and garlic. Mix with the beans, adding parsley, dill and pepper. Serve warm on a lettuce leaf as a first course.

Yield: About 3 cups

Cheese Strudel

6 sheets of filo or strudel dough, defrosted
½ cup melted butter
1 cup cheddar cheese, grated
½ cup cooked brown rice
½ cup fine bread crumbs
2 tablespoons finely chopped onion
Poppyseed (optional)

Keep filo dough covered with a damp towel to prevent leaves drying out. Separate leaves, brush each with melted butter, stacking until third leaf is buttered. Mix rice, cheese, crumbs and onion for filling, spread half of this on third leaf. Add 3 more leaves, buttering each layer. Spread remaining filling on top. Roll up like a jelly roll into a long oblong. Spread top with melted butter, sprinkle with poppy seeds if desired. Place on a buttered baking sheet. Cut through roll with a sharp knife, almost to the bottom leaf, to make separating into 12 pieces easier. Bake in a preheated 375° oven 25 to 30 minutes.

Serves 6

Potato Curls

1 large potato, peeled
Deep fat for frying
Parmesan cheese

Peel potato round and round as you would an apple, leaving strips a half inch wide. Keep these potato pieces covered with a damp towel to prevent browning. Heat oil to 365°. Drop in potato curls a few at a time, cooking a few minutes until they begin to brown. Remove and drain on paper towel. Sprinkle with parmesan cheese. Serve hot.

Yield: 2 servings

Zucchini Slices

1 medium size zucchini
1 clove garlic
2 tablespoons butter
2 tablespoons finely chopped parsley
2 ounces cheese, grated
paprika

Scrub zucchini, trim ends, slice about ⅓ inch thick. Put garlic through press and mash with butter and parsley. Spread onto slices, place on baking sheet. Top with grated cheese and sprinkle with paprika. Place under broiler for about 3 minutes until cheese is melted, serve hot.

Yield: About 24 slices

Stuffed Celery

1 bunch celery
1 8-ounce package of cream cheese, softened
2 tablespoons chopped green onions
2 tablespoons chopped parsley
1 teaspoon Worchestershire sauce
½ teaspoon paprika
2 tablespoons milk

Wash celery and cut inner ribs into 4 inch lengths. Blend cheese and remaining ingredients. Stuff the celery sticks. Serve cold.

Makes 16-18

Crustades and Fillings

12 slices very thinly sliced bread
¼ cup soft butter

Trim crusts from bread, rounding corners. Butter thinly.
Press gently into muffin cups. Bake at 350° about 10 minutes to
lightly brown.

Cool and fill.

Almond Filling

8 ounces cream cheese, softened
2 tablespoons milk
2 tablespoons chopped green onion
½ teaspoon Worchestershire sauce
2 tablespoons finely minced parsley
½ teaspoon paprika
½ cup toasted, slivered almonds

Mix all together and spoon into 12 crustade cups. Bake at 350° for
10 minutes and serve hot.

12 appetizers

Mushroom Filling

8 ounces fresh mushrooms, chopped
2 shallots, chopped
2 tablespoons butter
1 cup white sauce (page 98)
½ teaspoon rosemary

Clean and chop mushrooms. Cook with the shallots in melted
butter until lightly browned. Add to white sauce with the rosemary. Fill crustades. Bake at 350° for 10 minutes.

12 appetizers

Setting the Scene... *soups*

Vegetable Stock

This makes a good base for sauces and soups. Extra can be frozen in 1 cup containers.

¼ cup dried navy beans
¼ cup dried split green peas
1 medium onion, cut up
1 carrot, quartered
1 stalk celery, cut up
½ bunch parsley
¼ teaspoon ground mace
½ teaspoon thyme
Bouquet garni, or 1 bay leaf, 3 whole cloves, 3 peppercorns

Rinse dried beans and peas, place in heavy kettle, add 2 cups boiling water, cover and boil 5 minutes. Let sit for 30 minutes. Add vegetables, spices and 4 cups boiling water. Cover and simmer 1½ hours. Strain.

Yield: 1 quart

Green Lima Bean Soup

2 cups fresh baby green lima beans or 8 oz. frozen
1 cup boiling water
1 teaspoon powdered vegetable bouillion
½ teaspoon salt
1 cup milk

Cook fresh or frozen lima beans in boiling water with salt and vegetable stock for 15 to 20 minutes until tender. Add milk, puree in blender. Heat. Taste and add a little pepper. Serve with devilled crackers or herb toast (page 40).

Yield: 3 cups

Vegetable Soup

2 tablespoons butter or vegetable oil
1 cup onions, sliced
2 cups cabbage, sliced
3 carrots, sliced
2 stalks celery, sliced
1 medium turnip, sliced
2 potatoes, diced
1 bay leaf
¼ teaspoon thyme
salt and pepper to taste

Peel and dice the potatoes and cook in 2 cups of water 15 minutes. Heat a heavy bottomed kettle, add oil. Add onions, cabbage, carrots, celery and turnip and sauté, stirring occasionally, about 15 minutes. Add the potatoes with their cooking water. Add 6 cups of hot water, the bay leaf and thyme. Cover and simmer about 25 minutes. Remove bay leaf, add salt and pepper to taste.

Yield: 2½ quarts

Barley Soup

Instead of potatoes in vegetable soup recipe, cook ¼ cup pearl barley in 2 cups of water 40 minutes, then add to sautéed vegetables and cook until vegetables are tender.

Lentil Soup

1 cup lentils
1 tablespoon butter
½ medium onion
1 small carrot
1 stalk celery
1 bay leaf
4 cups boiling water
½ teaspoon salt
1 cup milk
1 tablespoon flour

Rinse the lentils well, drain. Melt the butter in a 2 quart saucepan. Add the cut up onion, carrot, celery and bay leaf. Cover and steam in butter about 10 minutes. Add the lentils, boiling water and salt, cover and simmer 30 to 40 minutes until the lentils are tender. Remove bay leaf. Cool a little, puree in a blender or processor. Return to pan. Add ⅔ cup of milk and bring to a simmer. Mix the flour with the remaining ⅓ cup milk and stir this into the soup slowly. Simmer about 5 more minutes. Taste and add salt and pepper if desired.

Serves 6

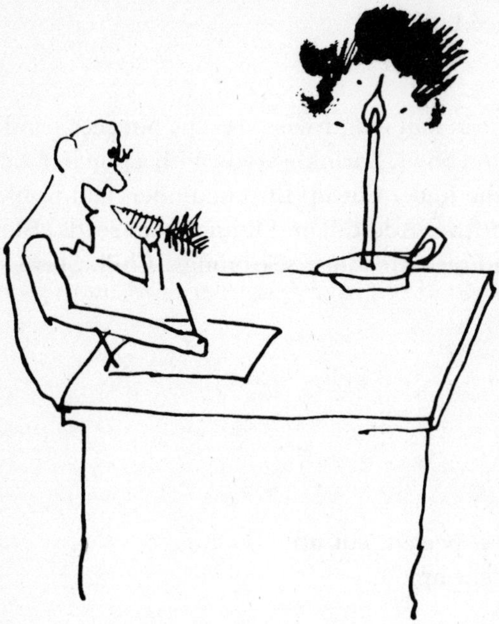

Cold Cucumber Soup

1 large cucumber
1 tablespoon green onions, chopped
2 tablespoons sour cream
½ teaspoon dill weed
Salt and pepper

Peel cucumber, cut in half lengthwise. Scrape out seeds and juice into a sieve set over a bowl. Sprinkle seeds with a pinch of salt and let drain, saving the juice. Cut up the cucumber, add to blender with onions, chop fine. Add dill and liquid from seeds. Blend in the sour cream and taste to adjust seasonings. Chill. Serve sprinkled with dill.

Serves 2

Potato Soup

4 medium potatoes, peeled, cut up
1 medium onion, cut up
3 cups water
1 teaspoon salt
1½ cups milk
2 tablespoons butter
2 tablespoons parsley, finely chopped

Cook the potatoes and onion in the salted water about 20 minutes, until tender. Mash slightly. Stir in the milk, but do not boil. Just before serving, swirl in the butter. Serve with parsley sprinkled on top.

Serves 4

Onion Soup

2 large onions, sliced
2 tablespoons butter
2 cups vegetable stock (page 32)
½ teaspoon Worcestershire sauce
2 tablespoons grated cheese
toast rounds

Sauté the sliced onions in the melted butter over low heat for 30 minutes, stirring occasionally. When onions are soft and golden, add stock, bring to simmer and cook covered for 30 minutes. Add Worcestershire sauce and taste before adding salt and pepper. To serve, place round of toast and grated cheese in each bowl before ladling hot soup over.

Serves 2

Tomato Soup

1 medium onion, sliced
4 tomatoes (about 1 pound), chopped
2 tablespoons butter
Bay leaf, few sprigs parsley
½ teaspoon salt
4 cups hot water
1 tablespoon quick-cooking tapioca
Croutons

Sauté the onion in butter until softened. Add the tomatoes, bay leaf, parsley and salt. Cover and simmer 15 minutes. Remove bay leaf and parsley, puree tomatoes and onions in blender. Return tomatoes to pan, add hot water and bring to a boil. Stir in the tapioca gradually and cook for 10 minutes longer. Serve with croutons.

Serves 4

Leek Soup

2 large leeks
1 large potato
¼ cup butter
2 cups boiling water
2 cups milk
Salt and pepper

Wash the leeks thoroughly, slice. Melt the butter in a saucepan and saute' the leeks a few minutes. Slice the potato thinly, add to leeks. Add 2 cups boiling water. Cover and cook very slowly, stirring occasionally, until soft. Add the milk and salt and pepper to taste. Puree in a blender, then return to pan to reheat.

Yield: 1 quart

Creamy Vegetable Soup

2 carrots
1 white turnip
1 medium onion
2 stalks celery
¼ cup butter
2 cups boiling water
2 cups milk
3 tablespoons flour
2 tablespoons chopped chives or parsley
Salt and pepper

Cut the vegetables into julienne strips. Melt the butter in a saucepan and sauté the vegetables until softened, about 10 minutes. Add the boiling water, cover and cook 5 minutes. Add 1½ cups of the milk and simmer until vegetables are tender. Season to taste. Mix the flour with the remaining milk and add slowly, stirring constantly as soup thickens. Serve hot garnished with chives or parsley.

Yield: 1 quart

Cheese Soup

2 tablespoons butter
¼ cup onion, chopped
¼ cup carrots, diced
¼ cup celery, diced
2 tablespoons flour
1 tablespoon cornstarch
½ teaspoon salt
¼ teaspoon dry mustard
⅛ teaspoon paprika
1 cup water
2 cups milk
½ cup cheddar cheese, diced

Melt butter, sauté onions until tender. Cook carrots and celery in 1 cup water 10 minutes. Add flour and cornstarch to onions, then add cooking water from carrots. Stir until liquid is thickened, add seasonings and milk. Stir until bubbly, add carrots and celery. Stir in the diced cheese last and cook slowly until cheese is melted. Serve sprinkled with chopped parsley or chives.

Yield: 1 quart

Tomato Consomme

1 pound fresh tomatoes or 1 15-oz. can stewed tomatoes
1½ cups water
½ teaspoon salt
1 teaspoon honey
1½ teaspoons cider vinegar
Cucumber or lemon slices for garnish

Peel and cut up fresh tomatoes, if used. Add water, salt and honey to tomatoes and simmer covered, about 30 minutes if fresh tomatoes, 10 minutes if canned are used. Add vinegar and puree in blender. Serve garnished with slice of cucumber or lemon.

Yield: 3 cups

soup accompaniments...

Devilled Crackers

¼ cup butter, softened
1 teaspoon prepared mustard
1 teaspoon curry powder
½ teaspoon Worchestershire sauce
few drops Tabasco or hot sauce

Cream these ingredients together and spread on thin crackers. Preheat oven to 400°. Place crackers on cookie sheet and bake for 3 to 4 minutes. Be careful they do not get too brown.

Herb Toast

½ loaf French bread, thinly sliced
¼ cup butter, softened
1 large garlic clove, pressed
¼ cup minced parsley
½ teaspoon dried basil or oregano

Combine butter with pressed garlic, parsley and basil or oregano. Spread thinly on bread slices. Place on baking sheet. Preheat oven to 375°, bake bread slices about 15 minutes until crisp. Serve hot, or store in air-tight tin and reheat before serving.

Croutons

2 slices whole wheat bread
2 tablespoons olive oil or melted butter

Cut bread into half-inch cubes, sprinkle with oil and bake on a sheet in a 350° oven 10 to 15 minutes until lightly browned and crisp. Store in covered jar.

Yield: 1 cup croutons

Entr'actes... *salads*

Spinach and Mushroom Salad

1 pound young spinach leaves
8 ounces mushrooms, sliced
2 hard-cooked eggs, (optional)

Wash spinach well, trim off tough ends. Drain, pat dry on towel. Tear up spinach, mix with mushrooms and toss with dressing. Garnish with sliced eggs if desired.

Dressing:
2 tablespoons cider vinegar
1 tablespoon lemon juice
1 tablespoon honey
2 teaspoons onions, finely chopped
½ cup vegetable oil
½ teaspoon dry mustard
½ teaspoon salt

Chop onions in blender, add vinegar, lemon juice, honey and seasonings. Add oil and blend well. Toss with spinach and mushrooms.

Serves 6

Cucumber and Yogurt Salad

2 cucumbers, peeled and thinly sliced
1 tablespoon finely chopped mint leaves
1 cup plain yogurt
Salt to taste

Blend mint leaves into yogurt, add cucumber slices and salt to taste. Sprinkle with chopped chives.

Serves 4

Cucumber and Dill Salad

1 medium cucumber, thinly sliced
1 small onion, thinly sliced
½ teaspoon salt
½ cup sour cream
1 teaspoon dill weed

Sprinkle salt on cucumber and onion slices, cover and chill 30 minutes. Drain, pressing out excess liquid. Mix with sour cream and dill, serve on lettuce leaves.

Serves 4

Avocado and Grapefruit Salad

1 avocado
2 grapefruit
few slices mild red onion
1 head Boston lettuce

Peel and slice avocado. Peel grapefruit and remove sections from membrane. Toss lettuce, avocado, grapefruit segments and onion slices with French dressing.

Serves 4

Coleslaw

2 ½ cups shredded cabbage
1 teaspoon salt
1 medium apple
1 medium carrot, grated
2 green onions, chopped
1 teaspoon minced parsley
3 tablespoons mayonnaise (page 54)
3 tablespoons sour cream
1 tablespoon cider vinegar
1 teaspoon honey

Sprinkle salt on cabbage, cover and let stand 15 minutes. Peel and chop apple. Mix mayonnaise, sour cream, vinegar and honey. Combine all ingredients, chill before serving.

Serves 6

Potato Salad

4 medium potatoes, boiled
¼ cup chopped onions
½ cup chopped celery
2 tablespoons finely chopped parsely
1 cup mayonnaise (page 54)
Salt and pepper

Slip skins from potatoes, cool and slice. Mix with onions, celery, parsley and mayonnaise. Add salt and pepper to taste. Sprinkle with paprika.

Serves 6

Avocado and Orange Salad

1 avocado
1 large orange
1 small head Bibb lettuce

Peel and slice avocado and orange. Arrange on lettuce leaves. Serve with mayonnaise or French dressing.

Serves 4

Crisp Cabbage and Raisin Salad

1 small head cabbage
1 cup golden raisins
1 8-ounce can sliced pineapple, drained
½ cup chopped walnuts

Remove outer leaves from cabbage and slice inner leaves thinly. Cut pineapple slices into sixths. Mix cabbage, raisins, pineapple and walnuts. Add dressing.

Dressing:
1 ½ cup milk or cream
1 teaspoon honey
⅛ teaspoon dry mustard
3 tablespoons lemon juice
¼ teaspoon salt
Paprika

Mix ingredients together with cabbage, sprinkle with paprika.

Serves 6

Russian Salad

1 cup cooked green peas
1 cup cooked diced potato
1 cup cooked green beans or carrots, diced
1 cup cooked diced beets
Mayonnaise to blend

Mix vegetables together, chill, bind with mayonnaise, or sour cream dressing (page 56).

Serves 6

Endive Salad Spanish Style

2 heads endive
2 large tomatoes
1 sweet red pepper, sliced
1 stalk celery, sliced
8 green and 8 black olives
French Dressing (page 53)

Wash and separate endive leaves, drain. Scald, peel and slice tomatoes. Arrange tomatoes on bed of endive, top with slices of red pepper, celery and garnish with olives. Pour dressing over to taste.

Serves 4

Garbanzo Bean Salad

1 15-ounce can garbanzo beans or chick peas, drained
2 green onions, chopped
1 tablespoon finely chopped parsley
1 4-ounce jar pimentos, drained, chopped
2 tablespoons olive oil
2 tablespoons white vinegar
½ teaspoon salt
⅛ teaspoon black pepper

Mix the beans, onions, parsley and pimentos. Blend oil, vinegar and seasonings. Stir beans and dressing together. Chill.

Serves 4

Tomatoes and Shallots

4 medium tomatoes
2 shallots, finely chopped
a few sprigs of parsley or watercress
French Dressing (page 53)
Fresh basil or ½ teaspoon dried

Scald, peel and slice tomatoes. Arrange in an overlapping circle on serving plate. Sprinkle with shallots. Top with French Dressing and fill center of plate with parsley or watercress. If fresh basil is available, add a few minced leaves to the dressing.

Serves 4

Stuffed Pepper Salad

1 medium green or sweet red pepper
½ cup grated Cheddar cheese
1 tablespoon chopped chutney (page 103)
1 tablespoon mayonnaise (page 54)
Lettuce

Cut pepper in half lengthwise and remove seeds and membrane. Mix cheese, chutney and mayonnaise. Fill green pepper halves with mixture. Serve on lettuce leaves.

Serves 2

Cream Cheese and Fruit Salad

4 peach or pear halves, or canned pineapple slices or plums
8 ounces softened cream cheese
1 cup finely chopped celery
½ cup chopped walnuts
Lettuce or endive leaves

Arrange lettuce and fruit on salad plates. Add cream cheese, sprinkle celery and nuts on each.

Dressing:
½ cup sour cream
2 tablespoons lemon juice
1 tablespoon honey

Mix together and pour over fruit and cheese salads.

Serves 4

Prune, Walnut and Cottage Cheese Salad

½ pound pitted prunes or 1 can plums
8 ounces cottage cheese
½ cup walnut halves
Lettuce

Pour boiling water over prunes, cover and let soften. Drain. Arrange lettuce on 8 plates, place prunes on lettuce, top with cottage cheese and then with walnuts. Serve with mayonnaise or French dressing.

Serves 8

Ginger Pear Molded Salad

1 16-ounce can pears
8 ounces cream cheese, softened
1 3-ounce package lime gelatin
½ teaspoon powdered ginger
  or 2 teaspoons chopped candied ginger

Drain pears, reserving juice. Bring 1 cup water to a boil, stir into gelatin. Measure pear can liquid and add enough water to make a cup. Add to hot gelatin mix. Blend in the cream cheese and ginger. Stir in the chopped pears. Chill until set. Unmold and serve on lettuce with mayonnaise.

Serves 6

Lime Cucumber Molded Salad

1 3-ounce package lime gelatin
¾ cup hot water
¼ cup lemon juice
1 teaspoon onion juice
½ cup mayonnaise (page 54)
½ cup sour cream
1 medium cucumber, peeled

Dissolve gelatin in hot water. Add lemon and onion juice. Chill until partially set. Grate the cucumber, using the large holes on the grater. Combine gelatin, cucumber. mayonnaise and sour cream. Chill until set, serve on lettuce.

Serves 4

Molded Grapefruit Salad

2 tablespoons (2 envelopes) unflavored gelatin
½ cup cold water
1 cup boiling water
⅓ cup sugar
1 17-ounce can grapefruit
1 ½ cups grapefruit juice
¼ cup pecans, broken

Soften gelatin in the cold water. Pour in boiling water and stir until gelatin is dissolved. Add sugar, stir well. Drain the grapefruit, reserving juice. Measure juice and add water to make 1 ½ cups. Add juice to gelatin and let partially set. Stir in the grapefruit sections and the pecans. Pour into an 8″ x 8″ pan. Chill. Cut into 6 squares to serve on lettuce with mayonnaise.
Garnish with pimento strips if desired.

Serves 6

Tomato Aspic Salad

2 tablespoons (2 envelopes) gelatin
½ cup cold water
2 cups tomato juice
1 medium onion, sliced
2 tablespoons vinegar
few sprigs parsley
Celery tops with leaves
1 bay leaf
4 whole cloves
1 teaspoon honey
½ teaspoon salt

Soften gelatin in the cold water, set aside. Cook the tomato juice with the onion, vinegar, parsley, celery and seasonings. Simmer slowly about 15 minutes. Strain and mix in the gelatin, stirring to dissolve. Pour into 6 individual ring molds. Optional additions before it sets are ½ cup sliced pimento stuffed olives or ½ cup chopped celery. Chill until firm, unmold on lettuce leaves and serve with mayonnaise.

Serves 6

salad dressings...

French Dressing

¼ cup vinegar
½ teaspoon honey
¼ teaspoon salt
¼ teaspoon paprika
6 tablespoons olive oil or vegetable oil
dash of black pepper

Combine all ingredients in a jar and shake well to blend.

Yield: about ½ cup

Curry Dressing: Add ½ teaspoon curry powder and shake well.

Cottage Cheese Dressing: Add 3 tablespoons cottage cheese and shake well.

Vinaigrette Dressing

2 tablespoons chopped green onions
2 tablespoons green pepper
2 tablespoons chopped parsley

Mix with French dressing and serve tossed with salad greens.

Herb Dressing

3 tablespoons cider vinegar
½ cup vegetable oil
⅛ teaspoon thyme
⅛ teaspoon marjoram
½ teaspoon salt
1 tablespoon chopped green onion
4 fresh basil or mint leaves, finely chopped (or use 1 teaspoon dried basil or mint)

Shake well together in a jar. Toss with salad greens.

About ⅔ cup

Mayonnaise

2 tablespoons lemon juice
½ teaspoon dry mustard
½ teaspoon salt
pinch of cayenne pepper
½ teaspoon honey (optional)
1 whole egg
½ cup vegetable oil or olive oil

Put all ingredients except oil into blender. Blend on high for a few seconds. Reduce speed, slowly add oil, blending as mayonnaise thickens.

Yield: ¾ cup

Chutney Dressing

Add 2 tablespoons chutney to mayonnaise recipe. Serve on cold vegetables.

Emerald Dressing

1 recipe mayonnaise
2 tablespoons finely chopped parsley
2 tablespoons green onions, chopped
½ teaspoon dried tarragon

Mix together and serve on wedges of lettuce.

Fruit Salad Dressing

1 recipe mayonnaise
½ cup dry roasted nuts, chopped
1 banana, cut up

Combine mayonnaise with nuts and banana and serve on cold fruit. Sprinkle coconut on top if desired.

Mustard Dressing

1 egg
1 tablespoon parmesan cheese
¼ teaspoon salt
2 tablespoons Dijon-type mustard
3 tablespoons lemon juice
1 teaspoon Worchestershire sauce
½ teaspoon honey
⅓ cup oil

Place all ingredients in blender except oil. Blend, then slowly add oil. Toss with spinach and other greens.

Russian Dressing

¾ cup mayonnaise (page 54)
2 tablespoons chili sauce
2 tablespoons chopped green pepper
1 tablespoon chopped onion

Mix ingredients together. Serve on wedges of lettuce.

Thousand Island Dressing

1 recipe Russian Dressing
2 hard cooked eggs

Chop eggs and fold into dressing. Serve on lettuce or cold cooked vegetables.

Sour Cream Dressing

½ cup sour cream
1 teaspoon prepared mustard
1 teaspoon honey
2 tablespoons lemon juice

Blend ingredients and serve on fruits or vegetables.

Sitting Room Only... *main dishes*

Carrot Croquettes

1 pound young carrots (7-8), cut up
1 small onion, chopped
⅛ teaspoon each mace, marjoram and thyme
½ teaspoon salt
½ cup white sauce (page 98)
1 egg, lightly beaten
Fine, dry bread crumbs
Vegetable oil for deep frying

Cook carrots and onion about 30 minutes until tender. Drain well and mash. Add herbs and salt. Blend in white sauce. Cool until firm, then shape into croquettes. Dip into egg, then roll in crumbs. Heat 3 inches of oil to 365 °, fry a few croquettes at a time 7 or 8 minutes until lightly browned. Lift out onto paper towels. Serve hot.

Yield: 12 croquettes

Bread and Cheese Puff

8 slices of bread
¼ cup butter, softened
1 cup grated cheese
3 eggs
2 cups milk
½ teaspoon salt

Butter a 9″ x 9″ pan. Trim crusts from bread, butter each slice. Alternate bread and cheese in layers. Beat eggs, add milk and salt and a dash of pepper. Pour over bread and cheese. Let stand for 1 hour or more. Place pan in a larger pan with 1″ of hot water in it. Bake in a 350° oven about 40-45 minutes. Serve at once.

Serves 6

Corn Pudding

1 17-ounce can whole kernel corn
1 17-ounce can cream style corn
3 eggs
1 cup milk
½ teaspoon salt
⅛ teaspoon black pepper

Drain the whole kernel corn. Beat eggs lightly, add milk and salt. Stir in the creamed corn and the whole kernels. Add salt and pepper. Pour into buttered 1 ½ quart baking dish. Bake at 350° about 40 minutes, until custard is set.

Serves 6

Cabbage Pie

1 double-crust recipe for pastry (page 119)
6 cups cabbage, shredded
3 tablespoons butter
1 teaspoon salt
⅛ teaspoon pepper
⅔ cup Cheddar cheese, grated

Roll out two crusts. Line a 9 inch pie plate with bottom crust. Melt butter in large skillet and saute the cabbage about 10 minutes until softened. Season cabbage with salt and pepper, stir in the cheese. Put cabbage into pie plate, top with other crust. Brush crust with milk and slash several times. Bake at 400° about 30 minutes until crust is lightly browned.

Serves 6

Cheese Fritters

1 egg
¾ cup milk
½ cup flour
½ teaspoon baking powder
½ teaspoon salt
½ cup sharp cheese, grated
Oil for deep frying

Lightly beat egg, add milk. Sift together the flour, baking powder and salt. Add to egg mixture, stir until smooth, add cheese. Heat 2 to 3 inches of vegetable oil to 365°. Drop in fritter batter by spoonful, a few at a time. Cook 3 to 4 minutes, turning to brown evenly.

Yield: about 14 fritters

Corn Fritters

1 egg, separated
1 cup fresh or frozen corn kernels
½ cup flour
1 teaspoon baking powder
½ teaspoon salt
¼ teaspoon cayenne pepper
¾ cup milk

Separate egg yolk from white. Beat yolk lightly, add milk, then dry ingredients and corn. Beat egg white and fold into batter. Heat 2 to 3 inches of oil to 365°. Drop in batter by spoonful, a few at a time. Cook 3 to 4 minutes, turning to brown evenly.

Yield: about 16 fritters

Curried Vegetables

3 medium potatoes
3 carrots
1 small white turnip
1 small cauliflower

Peel potatoes, carrots and turnip and cut into 1 inch cubes. Cook in lightly salted boiling water until tender. Break cauliflower into flowerets and cook until just tender. Drain all vegetables, then add to curry sauce.

Curry Sauce

1 medium onion
3 tablespoons butter
1 teaspoon curry powder
2 tablespoons flour
1 cup milk or vegetable stock
Salt and pepper to taste

Cut onion lengthwise into thin wedges and saute lightly in butter. Sprinkle with curry powder, cook a few minutes, add flour. Stir well to blend in, then add liquid. Cook until thickened, add salt and pepper to taste. Add the warm vegetables. Serve hot with rice.

Serves 4

Linguine and Mushrooms

12 oz. package linguine or thin spaghetti
1 medium onion, chopped
1 green pepper, chopped
3 tablespoons butter
2 tablespoons flour
1 cup mushrooms, sliced
1 cup milk
½ cup vegetable stock
½ teaspoon salt
⅛ teaspoon pepper
dash cayenne
3 tablespoons parmesan cheese

Cook pasta until tender, following instructions on package, drain. Saute onions and peppers in 2 tablespoons butter until softened. Sprinkle with flour, stir well. Add milk and vegetable stock, salt, pepper and cayenne. Cook until sauce thickens. Saute mushrooms in 1 tablespoon butter. Mix together pasta, sauce, mushrooms and cheese. Serve at once on a warm platter, garnish with a circle of cherry tomatoes that have been sauteed lightly in butter. Or place pasta mixture into a buttered 2-quart baking dish. Bake at 350° 15 to 20 minutes until edges bubble.

Serves 6

Noodles and Cottage Cheese

8 ounces thin noodles
1 cup sour cream
1 cup cottage cheese
6 green onions, chopped finely
1 clove garlic, chopped finely
¼ cup parsley, minced
¼ cup parmesan cheese
½ teaspoon salt
⅛ teaspoon pepper

Cook pasta until tender, drain. Mix with sour cream, cottage cheese, onions, garlic, parsley, cheese and seasonings. Turn into a buttered 2-quart casserole. Sprinkle with paprika. Bake at 350° about 30 minutes.

Serves 4

Macaroni and Cheese

2 cups elbow macaroni
¼ cup butter
¼ cup flour
2 cups milk
1 cup grated cheese
Salt and pepper to taste
¼ teaspoon dry mustard
⅛ teaspoon cayenne pepper
½ cup dry bread crumbs

Cook macaroni in 3 quarts of lightly salted boiling water until tender, drain well. Melt butter, stir in flour, cook a few minutes, then add milk. Cook until sauce is thickened, remove from heat and stir in cheese and seasonings. Add salt and pepper to taste. Turn into buttered 2-quart baking dish, top with bread crumbs and dot with butter. Bake at 375° for 20 minutes. Serve with broiled tomato slices.

Serves 4

Macaroni, Onion and Parsley Casserole

1 recipe Macaroni and Cheese (page 63)
1 clove garlic
8 green onions, finely chopped
1 cup parsley, finely chopped
2 tablespoons butter

Rub a small skillet with the cut clove of garlic. Heat the butter, add the chopped onions and sauté for 5 minutes. Add parsley and mix into the macaroni and cheese before baking.

Serves 4

Millet and Peas

1 cup uncooked millet
2 tablespoons butter
1 teaspoon salt
1 onion, chopped
3 cups boiling water
2 cups fresh peas, cooked or
   frozen peas, thawed
¼ cup toasted almonds, sliced

Place millet, butter, salt and onion in 2 quart sauce pan. Pour boiling water over, cover and simmer until liquid is absorbed, about 30 minutes. Stir in peas and almonds, cover, turn off heat. Keep covered 5 minutes to heat peas through.

Serves 4

Vegetable Charlotte

3 carrots
2 white turnips
½ pound Brussels sprouts
¼ cup butter
5 slices whole wheat bread

Butter a round one-quart dish. Cook each vegetable until tender in lightly salted water, drain and puree in blender or processor. Cut bread in half on the diagonal, butter on both sides. Using all but one slice, line baking dish with bread. Spoon in the pureed vegetables, swirl spoon through to mix vegetables but retain separate colors. Use remaining two triangles of bread for top of dish. Bake at 375° about 20 minutes.

Serve 6

Cabbage au Gratin

4 cups shredded cabbage
1 cup white sauce (page 98)
¼ cup grated cheese
¼ cup bread crumbs
2 tablespoons butter

Steam cabbage until tender, drain. Add to white sauce. Place in shallow buttered dish. Top with cheese, crumbs and dots of butter. Bake at 400 ° about 15 minutes or until lightly browned.

Serves 4

Eggplant au Gratin

1 medium eggplant
1 cup white sauce (recipe page 98)
¼ cup grated cheese
¼ cup bread crumbs
2 tablespoons butter

Peel and slice eggplant about ½ inch thick. Sprinkle with 1 teaspoon salt and cover. Let stand 30 minutes. Rinse. Mix ⅓ cup flour with ½ teaspoon paprika, pat each slice with flour. Pan fry in vegetable oil until lightly browned. Arrange in shallow baking dish, spread white sauce on top, then cheese and crumbs and dot with butter. Bake at 400° about 15 minutes.

Serves 4

Zucchini au Gratin

3 or 4 zucchini (about 1 pound)
1 cup white sauce (page 98)
¼ cup grated cheese
¼ cup bread crumbs
2 tablespoons butter

Wash zucchini, trim off ends. Slice ¾ inch thick and arrange in a buttered baking dish. Top with sauce, cheese and crumbs, dot with butter. Bake at 375 ° about 30 minutes.

Serves 4

Mushroom Tarts

8 2-inch tart shells or 4 4-inch pastry shells
8 ounces fresh mushrooms, sliced
1 cup white sauce (page 98)
2 tablespoons chopped onion
2 tablespoons chopped parsley
¼ teaspoon thyme
⅓ cup grated Swiss cheese
2 tablespoons butter

Rinse mushrooms, wipe dry and slice. Melt 1 tablespoon butter and saute mushrooms until lightly browned. Remove. Melt one tablespoon butter and sauté onion until tender. Add onion, parsley, thyme and cheese to white sauce. When cheese is melted, stir in mushrooms. Fill unbaked tart shells, place on baking sheet. Bake at 425° for 10 minutes, reduce heat to 375° and cook for 20 minutes more.

Serves 4

Cauliflower au Gratin

1 head cauliflower
1 cup white sauce (page 98)
¼ cup milk
⅓ cup grated cheese
¼ cup bread crumbs

Trim outer leaves and core from cauliflower and boil in lightly salted water until tender. Heat the white sauce, add the milk and cheese. Drain cauliflower, stand upright in dish, pour sauce over and top with bread crumbs. Bake in a hot oven (450°) about 5 minutes to lightly brown crumbs.

Serves 4

Hot Dutch Slaw

1 head cabbage
1 teaspoon salt
2 tablespoons butter
1 egg
2 teaspoons honey
⅛ teaspoon pepper
¼ cup vinegar

Remove outer leaves of cabbage and core. Shred inner leaves, making about 7 or 8 cups. Melt the butter in a heavy kettle over low heat, add cabbage and salt, cover and steam about 10 minutes, stirring once or twice. Beat the egg lightly, add the honey, pepper and vinegar. Pour this over the cabbage, stir and cook 5 minutes more.

Serves 6

Potato Mushroom Scallop

3 medium potatoes
¼ pound mushrooms
2 large onions
2 tomatoes
Salt and pepper
2 tablespoons butter

Peel and slice potatoes, onions and tomatoes. Wash and slice mushrooms. Arrange potatoes, onions and mushrooms in a buttered 2 quart casserole in layers, sprinkling lightly with salt and pepper. Top with the sliced tomatoes. Dot with butter. Cover casserole and bake for 50-60 minutes at 350 °.

Serves 4

Potatoes Gratin

2 large potatoes
2 eggs
¼ cup milk
¼ teaspoon salt
1 clove garlic
2 tablespoons minced chives (optional)
½ cup Swiss cheese, grated
2 tablespoons butter

Peel and grate the potatoes, using the large holes of the grater. Squeeze out in a towel. Rub a 9 inch pie plate with a cut clove of garlic, heat the plate with the 2 tablespoons of butter until butter is foamy. Beat the eggs, add milk, salt, potatoes and chives. Place in pie plate, top with cheese and bake at 375° for 30 minutes. Cut in wedges to serve.

Serves 6

Risotto

2 tablespoons butter
1 small onion, chopped
1 cup brown rice
2 ½ cups water
1 teaspoon powdered vegetable bouillion
½ teaspoon salt

Sauté the onion in the melted butter until softened. Add the rice, then liquid and seasonings. Cover the pan and cook over medium low heat 40 to 45 minutes, until the liquid is absorbed.

Serves 4

Risotto with Peas

Cook rice as above. About 5 minutes before rice is finished cooking, stir in a 10-ounce package of frozen green peas. Cover and continue cooking until peas are heated through and rice is tender. Sprinkle with ¼ cup grated Parmesan cheese.

Serves 4

Green Rice

Add 1 cup chopped fresh spinach during the last 5 minutes of cooking time or fold in ½ cup finely chopped parsley after rice is tender.

Serves 4

Vegetable Fried Rice

1 onion, sliced
1 green pepper, cut in thin strips
1 carrot, thinly sliced
1 cup cabbage, thinly sliced
1 cup mushrooms, sliced
¼ pound fresh bean sprouts
   or 1 8-ounce can water chestnuts, drained, sliced
2 cups cooked rice
3 tablespoons oil
2 eggs
2 tablespoons soy sauce
4 green onions, cut in ½ inch lengths

Heat the oil in a large skillet or wok. Add the onions, pepper strips, carrots and cabbage and stir fry for 5 minutes. Add mushrooms, cook a few minutes, then add the rice. Mix well, cover and cook 5 minutes over low heat. Add the bean sprouts or water chestnuts and the soy sauce. Make a hollow in the center of the rice, drop in the eggs and stir with a fork until they are lightly cooked, then stir eggs into the rice and vegetables. Sprinkle green onions on top and serve hot.

Serves 4

Savory Rice

1 cup brown rice
3 tablespoons olive oil
2 cloves garlic, minced
1 large onion, chopped
1 green pepper, chopped
1 teaspoon salt
¼ teaspoon black pepper
⅛ teaspoon cayenne pepper
3 cups tomato juice (or 1 6-oz. can tomato paste plus water to make
   3 cups liquid)

Heat pan with olive oil, add chopped garlic, onions and peppers.
Sauté 5 minutes, add rice, sauté a few minutes more. Add salt,
pepper and liquid, cover pan and cook 40 to 45 minutes until rice
is tender and liquid is absorbed.

Serves 4

Stuffed Egg Casserole

8 stuffed egg halves (see page 24)
1 cup white sauce (see page 98)
¼ cup bread crumbs
2 tablespoons butter
Paprika

Butter a shallow baking dish and arrange stuffed eggs. Spoon
white sauce over eggs. Sprinkle with bread crumbs and paprika
and dot with butter. Bake at 350° about 20 minutes. Serve eggs on
buttered toast cut into triangles.

Serves 4

Savory Eggplant

1 medium eggplant
½ teaspoon salt
3 tablespoons flour
1 teaspoon paprika
⅛ teaspoon pepper
¼ cup olive oil
1 large onion, sliced
1 green pepper, sliced
1 large tomato, sliced

Peel eggplant and slice about ½ inch thick. Sprinkle with salt, cover and let stand about 30 minutes. Rinse eggplant slices and dry on paper towels. Mix flour, salt, paprika and pepper. Dip each slice into seasoned flour, then fry in 3 tablespoons of the olive oil. Remove eggplant, keep warm. Heat remaining tablespoon of oil in skillet and lightly sauté the onion and pepper slices. In a 6-cup baking dish, layer eggplant, onions, peppers and top with the sliced tomatoes. Cover and bake at 375° for 20 minutes. This is also good served cold as a first course.

Serves 4

Shepherds Pie

½ cup dried white lima beans
2 onions
2 carrots
2 stalks celery
1 white turnip
1 cup white sauce (page 98)
½ teaspoon thyme
⅛ teaspoon pepper
1 tablespoon chopped parsley
2 large potatoes
¼ cup milk
1 tablespoon butter
Paprika

Wash the beans, rinse, cover with 1 ½ cups water, bring to a boil and cook uncovered for 2 minutes. Let stand for 1 hour. Cook beans until tender. Peel and cut up onions, carrots and cook them in lightly salted water until tender. Drain the beans and use any liquid to add to milk for making the white sauce. Cook and mash the potatoes with the milk and butter. Place vegetables in a buttered baking dish, adding chopped celery and minced parsley. Stir in the white sauce, seasoned with thyme and pepper. Heap the mashed potatoes on top and sprinkle with paprika. Bake at 375° 20 to 25 minutes until top is lightly browned.

Serves 4

souffles...

Successful souffles result from following a few basic rules. Using the right size mold, a straight-sided round baking dish, approximately 3 inches high, 7 1/2 inches across, is right for 4 to 5 cups of a mixture. The dish needs to be well buttered on bottom and sides. Fine dry bread crumbs or parmesan cheese may be rolled around the inside and excess crumbs shaken out. Eggs should be at room temperature. The yolks are added to the slightly cooled sauce, the whites beaten until they form peaks, then gently folded into the mixture. Preheat the oven to 400°, place the souffle on the middle rack and immediately reduce the temperature to 375°. Don't open the oven door for 20 minutes. After 30 minutes, the souffle will have puffed up and the top will be lightly browned. Turn off heat, leave souffle in the oven 5 minutes more, then serve at once.

Walnut Onion Souffle

4 onions, sliced
1 cup milk
3 tablespoons butter
1/4 cup flour
1 teaspoon salt
1/8 teaspoon pepper
1/2 cup walnuts, chopped
1 tablespoon minced parsley
5 egg yolks
5 egg whites

Pour the milk over the sliced onions, cover pan and cook slowly until onions are soft. Drain liquid to use in sauce, adding more milk if there is less than 1 1/4 cups. Melt the butter, stir in the flour, cook a few minutes before adding salt, pepper and milk. Stir until thick and bubbling. Add onions, walnuts and egg yolks. Preheat oven. Beat egg whites until peaks form, fold gently into sauce. Pour into prepared souffle dish and bake at 375° for 30 minutes.

Serves 6

Broccoli or Cauliflower Souffle

1 pound cauliflower or broccoli
3 tablespoons butter
¼ cup flour
1 ½ cups milk
½ teaspoon salt
4 large eggs, separated

Separate vegetables into flowerets, cook in boiling water 10 minutes, drain. Make a sauce by melting butter, adding flour, cook a few minutes, then add milk and salt and cook until thick and bubbling. Cool slightly, stir in the egg yolks and the vegetables. Whip the egg whites until peaks form, then fold gently into the sauce. Preheat oven. Place in prepared souffle dish (see page 75) and bake at 375° for 30 minutes.

Serves 4

Cheese Souffle

¼ cup butter
¼ cup flour
1 ½ cups milk
¼ teaspoon dry mustard
½ teaspoon salt
pinch of cayenne pepper
4 eggs, separated
1 ½ cups sharp Cheddar cheese, grated

Make a roux of butter and flour, add mustard and pepper. Add milk and cook until thickened, remove from heat and stir in cheese. When cheese is melted and mixture slightly cooled, stir in the egg yolks. Preheat oven. Beat the whites until soft peaks form. Then fold in the whites, and bake at 375° for 30 to 40 minutes.

Serves 4

Mushroom Souffle

¼ cup plus 2 tablespoons butter
¼ cup flour
1 ½ cup milk
½ teaspoon salt
⅛ teaspoon black pepper
8 ounces fresh mushrooms, sliced

Make a white sauce of ¼ cup butter, flour and milk. Add salt and pepper. Beat egg yolks lightly. Saute the mushrooms in 2 tablespoons hot butter until lightly browned. Stir into the white sauce before adding egg yolks. Preheat oven. Beat the whites until soft peaks form. Fold in the beaten whites and bake at 375°for 30 to 40 minutes.

Serves 4

Spinach Souffle: Replace mushrooms with 1 pound fresh spinach leaves

Wash spinach, trimming tough stems. Place in pan with just the water clinging to the leaves, cover and steam for 5 minutes. Drain and chop. Add spinach to white sauce with ¼ teaspoon nutmeg. Add yolks, then beaten whites and bake as directed.

Stuffed Eggplant

2 one-pound eggplants
1 clove garlic, minced
1 onion, chopped
1 green pepper, chopped
2 tablespoons vegetable oil
½ teaspoon salt
⅛ teaspoon pepper
½ teaspoon basil
½ teaspoon oregano
2 tomatoes, chopped (or 1 small can tomato sauce)
2 tablespoons minced parsley
½ cup bread crumbs
2 tablespoons parmesan cheese (optional)

Cut eggplant lengthwise into two halves. Cook in a small amount of boiling water for 10 minutes. Drain, scoop out centers, leaving one-half inch of shell. Chop the removed eggplant. Heat the oil in a skillet, sauté the garlic, onion and green pepper 5 minutes, add chopped eggplant and cook 5 minutes more. Mix with the tomatoes, parsley and seasonings. Fill the shells. Top each with crumbs and cheese. Bake at 375° for 30 minutes.

Serves 4

Stuffed Green Peppers

2 large green peppers
1 large onion, chopped
2 tablespoons vegetable oil
2 cups cooked rice
½ teaspoon basil
½ teaspoon oregano
1 16-ounce can tomatoes
Salt and pepper to taste
1 teaspoon honey

Cut peppers in half lengthwise, remove membranes and seeds. Parboil for 5 minutes in lightly salted water, drain. Sauté onions in oil until softened. Divide tomatoes in half. Mix together the rice, seasonings and half the tomatoes. Add salt and pepper to taste. Stuff shells. Puree the remaining tomatoes, adding the honey. Spoon this sauce over tops of stuffed peppers. Place in a buttered shallow baking dish and bake at 375° about 30 minutes.

Serves 4

Stuffed Tomatoes

4 tomatoes
1 shallot, chopped
1 tablespoon butter
1 tablespoon parsley, chopped
3 tablespoons fresh basil, chopped, or 1 tablespoon dried basil
½ teaspoon salt
⅛ teaspoon pepper
½ cup bread crumbs

Slice the top off each tomato and scoop out the meat, discarding seeds if desired. Sauté the shallot in butter until softened. Mix chopped tomato pulp, shallot, parsley, basil, salt and pepper. Spoon into shells. Top with the bread crumbs, dot with additional butter. Place in a baking dish and bake at 375° 15 minutes until tops brown.

Serves 4

Stuffed Onions

4 large flattish onions (flat onions are sweeter than elongated ones)
¼ cup slivered almonds
2 tablespoons dry bread crumbs
3 tablespoons melted butter
½ teaspoon salt
⅛ teaspoon pepper
¼ cup grated cheese

Peel onions. To keep them from separating, cut a cross in the stem end of each. Cook in boiling salted water about 5 minutes. Lift out carefully, drain. Remove the centers, leaving a shell. Chop removed onion, add almonds, crumbs, butter, salt and pepper. Stuff onions, top with grated cheese. Place in buttered baking dish. Bake at 375° for 20 minutes.

Serves 4

Stuffed Zucchini

4 medium zucchini (5 to 6 inches long)
1 clove garlic, chopped
2 tablespoons vegetable oil
½ cup walnuts, chopped
1 teaspoon salt
⅛ teaspoon pepper
¼ teaspoon sage
¼ cup Swiss cheese, grated

Trim ends from zucchini, cook in boiling water for 5 minutes. Drain, cut in half lengthwise. Scoop out pulp, leaving a shell. Chop pulp. Sauté the onion in oil, add pulp, cook a few minutes. Add walnuts and seasonings, stuff shells. Top with grated cheese. Place in a buttered baking pan, add ¼ cup hot water around shells. Bake at 350° for 25 minutes.

Serves 4

Pinto Bean and Cornbread Pie

1 30-ounce can chili pinto beans
1 medium onion, chopped
1 green pepper, chopped
2 tablespoons olive oil
1 cup corn meal
1 egg
1 cup milk
1 tablespoon oil
1 teaspoon chili powder
½ teaspoon salt

Sauté onions and pepper in olive oil until softened. Mix with beans and pour into 9 inch pie plate. Lightly beat egg and milk, add corn meal, salt, chili powder and 1 tablespoon oil. Pour over beans. Bake at 375° 30 minutes. Cut in wedges to serve.

Serves 6

Red Cabbage and Apples

1 pound red cabbage
1 small onion, chopped
1 apple, sliced thinly
1 tablespoon vinegar
1 tablespoon honey
½ teaspoon salt
¼ cup water
2 tablespoons butter

Remove outer leaves from cabbage and shred inner leaves. Melt butter in sauce pan, add onion, cook a few minutes. Add cabbage, stir to coat well with butter, then add other ingredients, stir, cover pan and cook over low heat about 15 minutes. Stir once or twice.

Serves 6

Summer Squash Medley

2 small green zucchini
2 small yellow squash
1 medium onion, sliced
2 cloves garlic, minced
2 tablespoons butter
½ teaspoon salt
⅛ teaspoon pepper
1 teaspoon dried rosemary, crumbled

Wash and trim squash but do not peel. Cut into julienne sticks about 2″ long. Heat pan, melt butter, add onions and garlic. Cook 2 minutes, then stir in squash. Cover and cook over low heat about 5 to 7 minutes, don't overcook. Season with salt, pepper and rosemary.

Serves 4

Baked Onions

2 cups sliced onions (2 to 3 onions)
2 tablespoons butter
4 slices buttered toast
1 cup cheese, grated
1 egg
⅔ cup milk
½ teaspoon salt
⅛ teaspoon pepper

Melt butter in a skillet and sauté the onions 10 to 15 minutes over medium low heat. Cut toast into half inch cubes. In a 1 ½ quart buttered baking dish, layer the toast, onions and cheese. Mix egg, milk, salt and pepper. Pour over the onions. Cover and let stand for several hours. Bake at 375° for 30 minutes.

Serves 6

Beets in Orange Sauce

½ cup orange juice
2 tablespoons lemon juice
1 tablespoon vinegar
½ teaspoon salt
1 tablespoon honey
1 tablespoon cornstarch
2 tablespoons cold water
2 tablespoons butter
1 17-ounce can tiny whole beets or sliced beets

Mix in small sauce pan the orange and lemon juice, vinegar, salt and honey. Stir cornstarch into cold water and add to pan. Cook this over low heat, stirring, until sauce bubbles. Drain the beets. Stir the butter into the sauce, add the beets and heat thoroughly.

Serves 4

Glazed Butternut Squash

1 ½ pounds butternut squash
¼ cup honey
½ teaspoon cinnamon
¼ teaspoon nutmeg
¼ cup butter, melted

Peel and seed the squash, cut into ½ inch cubes. Steam until tender, about 10-12 minutes. Drain well. Melt butter, adding honey and spices. Place squash in 1 quart buttered baking dish, drizzle butter-honey mixture over squash. Bake at 400° about 15 minutes.

Serves 4

Lemon Cabbage

4 cups cabbage, thinly sliced
2 tablespoons butter
1 lemon
½ teaspoon salt
⅛ teaspoon pepper
¼ cup water

Melt butter in heavy skillet, add cabbage, stir and cook a few minutes. Grate ½ teaspoon of lemon rind, sprinkle over cabbage with the salt and pepper. Add the juice of the lemon and the water. Cover and simmer over low heat about 10 minutes until cabbage is tender but crisp.

Serves 4

Sweet Potatoes and Walnuts

2 large sweet potatoes
1 tablespoon butter
1 tablespoon honey
¼ teaspoon salt
¼ teaspoon nutmeg
½ cup walnuts or pecans, chopped

Peel potatoes and steam until tender. Drain and mash, adding butter, honey, salt and nutmeg. Place in buttered pie plate or baking dish, sprinkle top with walnuts. Bake at 350° 20 minutes.

Serves 4

Walnut Cheese Balls

1 cup walnuts
1 cup bread crumbs
½ cup grated Swiss cheese
¼ cup onion, minced
2 tablespoons parsley, minced
2 eggs, lightly beaten
¼ teaspoon salt
⅛ teaspoon pepper

Chop walnuts in blender. Beat eggs lightly, add walnuts, crumbs, cheese, onion, parsley and seasonings. Roll mixture into balls the size of large walnuts. Arrange in a 6″ x 9″ buttered baking dish. Pour over:
1 cup white sauce (page 98)
¼ teaspoon thyme
Bake at 375° about 25-30 minutes.

Yield: 12 balls

Brussels Sprouts with Almonds

1 pound Brussels sprouts
3 tablespoons butter
½ cup sliced almonds

Trim outer leaves from Brussels sprouts, cut a small cross in base. Cook in lightly salted water until tender, 15 to 20 minutes. Drain. Melt butter in pan, add the almonds and sauté a few minutes, pour over the sprouts.

Serves 4

Green Beans with Onion

1 pound young tender green beans
1 medium onion, sliced
3 tablespoons butter
Salt, pepper and paprika

Wash beans and trim ends. Bring 2 quarts of lightly salted water to a boil and add beans. Cover and cook 8 to 10 minutes in rapidly boiling water, until beans are tender but crisp. Drain. Melt the butter in a small skillet, add the sliced onion and cook 10 minutes. Combine beans and sauteed onions, sprinkle with black pepper and paprika.

Serves 4

Lentil and Rice Roast

2 cups cooked lentils
1 cup brown rice
2 onions, chopped
½ cup celery, chopped
1 cup fresh whole wheat bread crumbs
1 cup pecans, chopped
1 teaspoon thyme
½ teaspoon sage
1 teaspoon salt
¼ teaspoon black pepper
¼ cup butter

Melt butter in saucepan and sauté onions and celery until crisp-tender. Cook the rice 40 to 45 minutes in 3 cups water. Mix together the lentils, rice, onion, crumbs, nuts and seasonings. Place in a buttered 2-quart casserole dish and bake 40 minutes at 350°. Serve with brown sauce.

Serves 6

Lentil Curry

1 cup lentils
½ teaspoon salt
2 onions, chopped
2 bananas, sliced
1 teaspoon honey
1 teaspoon curry powder
1 tablespoon lemon juice
⅓ cup raisins
1 ½ cup rice
¼ cup shredded coconut
Chutney (page 102)

Wash the lentils and cook in 3 cups lightly salted water about 35 minutes until tender. Add onions, apples, bananas, honey, curry powder, lemon juice and raisins and cook 15 minutes more. Meanwhile, cook the brown rice in 3 ½ cups water until tender and liquid is absorbed. Arrange rice in a ring on the serving platter, fill center with lentil curry, top with coconut. Serve with chutney.

Serves 6

Green Split Pea Curry

1 cup dried green split peas
2 ½ cups water
1 teaspoon salt
2 young carrots, sliced
1 medium onion, sliced
1 tablespoon vegetable oil
1 teaspoon curry powder
1 teaspoon tumeric

Rinse the dried peas, place in pan with water, add salt, bring to a boil, add sliced carrots, cover and simmer 40 to 45 minutes until tender. Sauté onion in oil 5 minutes, add curry powder and tumeric and cook 5 minutes more. Stir onions into peas. Serve over rice with chutney.

Serves 4

Curried Rice and Tomatoes

1 cup brown rice
1 large apple, chopped
1 onion, chopped
2 tablespoons butter
1 teaspoon curry powder
2 tablespoons flour
½ teaspoon salt
1 cup milk
1 8-ounce can tomato sauce
2 tomatoes, cut in half
Chopped parsley
Chutney

Cook the rice in 2 ½ cups lightly salted water about 40 minutes until tender. Sauté the apple and onion in the butter about 10 minutes, sprinkle with curry powder, cook 5 minutes more. Add flour, stir in well, then add milk and tomato sauce and cook until sauce is thickened. Place tomato halves under broiler for 5 minutes to grill. Combine cooked rice with sauce, top with tomato halves and chopped parsley. Serve with chutney.

Serves 4

Scallopped Tomatoes

1 pound fresh tomatoes or 1 16-ounce can of tomatoes
2 slices of bread, diced
½ teaspoon salt
1 teaspoon honey
⅛ teaspoon pepper
2 tablespoons butter

If using fresh tomatoes, peel and cut up. Into 1-quart buttered dish, combine tomatoes, bread cubes, salt, honey and pepper. Dot top with bits of butter. Bake at 375° for 20 minutes.

Serves 4

Vegetable Deep Dish Pie

1 large onion, cut in wedges
2 carrots, cut in 1 inch chunks
2 white turnips, diced
1 large potato, diced
1 10-oz. package frozen peas, thawed
2 cups white sauce (page 98)
¼ teaspoon thyme
1 recipe single crust pastry (page 119)

Cook the onion, carrots, turnip, potato in lightly salted water until tender, drain, mix with peas and white sauce. Pour into round 1 ½ quart casserole, top with pie crust. Slash crust several times. Preheat oven. Bake at 425° for 10 minutes, reduce heat to 375° and bake 20 minutes more until crust is lightly browned.

Serves 6

Vegetables in Puff Pastry

1 10-ounce package frozen patty shells
Vegetable and sauce mixture as in deep dish pie recipe above.

Bake patty shells according to directions on box, fill with vegetable mixture and serve hot.

Serves 6

Sweet Pepper Pie

One single crust pastry (page 119)
1 sweet red pepper
1 green bell pepper
1 onion, sliced
1 tablespoon butter
3 eggs
1 ½ cups milk
1 teaspoon salt
½ cup Swiss cheese, grated

Remove seeds and membrane from peppers, slice. Melt butter in skillet and sauté onion and peppers 10 to 15 minutes to soften. Place unbaked pastry in 9 inch pie pan. Preheat oven. Whisk eggs, milk and salt together, stir in cheese. Put peppers and onions in pie shell, pour egg mixture over. Bake at 425° for 20 minutes, then reduce heat to 350° and bake 20 to 25 minutes more, until a knife inserted in the center comes out clean.

Serves 6

Vegetable Macedoine

2 carrots
1 white turnip
1 onion, cut in wedges
1 cup fresh or frozen peas
1 cup Supreme sauce (page 99)
pinch of mace
4 slices buttered toast

Cut carrots and turnip into thin julienne strips. Cook in lightly salted water, with the onion, until tender. Cook the peas. Prepare the Supreme sauce, add mace. Stir the vegetables into the sauce. Cut toast into triangles. Serve vegetables on the toast points.

Serves 4

Potato Nut Patties

½ cup chopped mixed nuts
2 large potatoes
⅓ cup milk
½ teaspoon salt
⅛ teaspoon pepper
1 teaspoon minced onion
¼ cup bread crumbs
1 egg

Cook and mash the potatoes, adding milk, salt and pepper. Combine with the nuts, onion, crumbs and egg and cool the mixture until firm. Shape into 8 patties. Lightly beat 1 egg and have additional crumbs ready. Dip patties in egg and then in crumbs. Pan fry in a small amount of vegetable oil until brown, turning once.

Serves 4

New Potatoes and Peas in Dill Sauce

1 pound small red new potatoes
2 cups fresh peas or 10-ounce package frozen peas
1 cup white sauce (page 98)
2 teaspoons dried dill weed (or 2 tablespoons fresh dill)

Wash and partially peel potatoes, removing a half inch band of skin around center of each. Cook in boiling, lightly salted water until tender, drain. Prepare the white sauce and add dill. Cook peas until tender, combine potatoes, peas and sauce.

Serves 4

Cheese and Potato Pie

3 large potatoes
½ cup milk
Salt and pepper to taste
1 cup Cheddar cheese, grated
1 egg, lightly beaten
2 tablespoons butter

Cook potatoes until tender, drain and mash, adding milk, salt and pepper to taste, grated cheese, butter and egg. Heap into a buttered 9 inch pie plate. Bake for 30 minutes at 375°.

Serves 4

Potato Pancakes

3 medium potatoes
2 tablespoons grated onion
2 tablespoons flour
½ teaspoon salt
⅛ teaspoon pepper
¼ cup vegetable oil

Wash and grate the potatoes, keeping covered with wet cloth to avoid discoloration. Press in sieve to drain excess water. Mix with grated onion, flour and seasonings. heat oil in skillet, drop on tablespoonsful of pancake mixture, fry on both sides until browned.

Makes 12 pancakes

Nut Cutlets

1 cup walnuts or pecans, chopped
2 tablespoons butter
1 small onion, chopped
2 tablespoons flour
⅔ cup milk
2 cups fresh whole wheat bread crumbs
1 egg
Salt and pepper to taste
¼ teaspoon thyme

Sauté the onion in the melted butter until tender. Add the flour, then stir in the milk and cook until thick. Add other ingredients and lightly beaten egg. Chill the mixture. Shape into 8 cutlets. Pat with a little flour, then fry in a little hot vegetable oil until brown, turning once.

Serves 4

Nut and Rice Roast

1 cup cooked brown rice
1 cup walnuts or pecans, chopped
1 cup fresh whole wheat bread crumbs
1 large onion, chopped
2 tablespoons butter
1 teaspoon salt
½ teaspoon sage
½ teaspoon thyme
⅛ teaspoon pepper
¼ teaspoon dry mustard
Cumberland Sauce (page 100)

Combine rice, nuts, crumbs, onion, butter and seasonings. Place in small buttered loaf pan. Bake at 375° for 30 minutes. Serve with Cumberland Sauce.

Serves 4

The Plot Thickens... *sauces*

White Sauce

2 tablespoons butter
2 tablespoons flour
¼ teaspoon salt
1 cup milk

Melt the butter in a saucepan. Add the flour, stir vigorously with a whisk to form a roux. Cook for 1 minute, then slowly add milk, whisking to keep smooth. Cook over low heat, whisking, until it begins to bubble.

Yield: 1 cup

Celery Sauce

1 cup chopped celery
1 cup white sauce

Cover celery with boiling water and cook 5 minutes, covered. Drain, add to white sauce.

Yield: about 1½ cups

Cheese Sauce

1 cup white sauce
½ cup grated Cheddar cheese
¼ teaspoon dry mustard
⅛ teaspoon black pepper

Add cheese, mustard and pepper to white sauce. Cook until cheese is melted.

Mushroom Sauce

1 cup white sauce
1 cup mushrooms, sliced
1 tablespoon butter

Melt butter in small skillet, add sliced mushrooms and cook over medium heat until mushrooms are lightly browned. Add with pan liquids to the white sauce.

Parsley Sauce

1 cup white sauce
¼ cup finely chopped parsley

Add the parsley to the white sauce and heat.

Supreme Sauce

1 cup white sauce
1 egg, lightly beaten
2 tablespoons lemon juice

Pour some of the white sauce over the lightly beaten egg, add the lemon juice, combine with the remaining white sauce and cook over low heat 3 to 4 minutes.

Caper Sauce

1 cup white sauce
2 tablespoons capers, drained
1 tablespoon lemon juice

Add capers and juice to white sauce and heat.

Cranberry Orange Relish

2 cups fresh cranberries
½ large orange
1 apple
3 tablespoons honey

Remove seeds from orange, cut up some of the peel. Cut apple into chunks, removing core and seeds. In processor, chop cranberries, apple and orange with peel. Add the honey, blend. Chill.

Yield: 2½ cups

Cranberry Sauce

2 cups fresh cranberries
½ cup water
3 to 4 tablespoons honey

Add water to cranberries and cook over medium high heat until skins begin to pop. Reduce heat, add honey, and cook slowly, uncovered, about 10 minutes, stirring occasionally, until sauce has thickened and berries are tender.

Yield: About 2 cups

Cumberland Sauce

½ cup orange juice
2 tablespoons red currant jelly
¼ teaspoon dry mustard
pinch of cayenne pepper
1 teaspoon grated orange peel

Combine ingredients in small sauce pan and heat until jelly is melted.

Yield: about ½ cup

Hollandaise Sauce

¼ cup butter, softened
3 egg yolks
1 teaspoon cornstarch
2 tablespoons lemon juice
½ teaspoon salt
1 cup boiling water
pinch cayenne pepper

Beat the yolks into the butter. Add cornstarch to lemon juice. Add to yolks, add salt and pepper. Put pan over low heat and slowly whisk in the boiling water. Blend well but do not overcook.

Yield: 1 cup

Bernaise Sauce

1 cup Hollandaise sauce
¼ cup parsley, finely chopped
2 tablespoons shallot, finely chopped
½ teaspoon dried tarragon
1 tablespoon white vinegar

Cook shallot in vinegar over low heat until tender. Add tarragon and parsley. Add Hollandaise sauce and heat.

Yield: 1 cup

Fresh Tomato Sauce

3 ripe tomatoes, scalded, peeled and chopped
3 shallots or green onions, chopped
1 teaspoon honey
1 bay leaf
½ cup vegetable stock or Brown Sauce

Put tomatoes, shallots, honey and bay leaf in sauce pan. Simmer about 15 minutes, covered. Remove the bay leaf, puree tomaoes in blender. Return to pan, add stock or sauce, heat. Taste and add pepper and salt if needed.

Yield: About 1½ cups

Green Tomato Chutney

3 pounds green tomatoes, chopped
1 medium onion, chopped
2 pounds apples, peeled, chopped
½ cup honey
1½ cups cider vinegar
1 teaspoon fresh ginger root, chopped
1 cup raisins or currants
1 teaspoon mustard seed
1 teaspoon ground allspice
½ teaspoon dried red pepper flakes
½ cup walnuts, chopped

In a heavy 4 quart kettle, place all ingredients except walnuts. Bring to a boil and cook over low heat, stirring occasionally, not covered, for about 2½ hours. Mixture will cook down and darken. Add walnuts last 5 minutes. Pack while hot into sterilized jars and seal immediately.

Yield: 8 half-pint jars

Spicy Sauce

1 tomato, scalded, peeled and chopped
1 teaspoon butter
1 cup Brown Sauce (page 104)
1 tablespoon cider vinegar
¼ teaspoon dry mustard
1 teaspoon Worcestershire sauce
1 tablespoon chutney, chopped

Saute the tomato in the melted butter for 10 minutes. Add other ingredients and simmer about 10 to 15 minutes.

Yield: About 1 cup

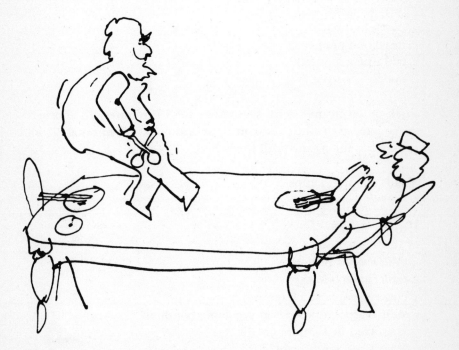

Apple Sauce

3 cooking apples
2 tablespoons water
1 teaspoon lemon juice
1 teaspoon honey

Peel apples, remove cores and seeds. Cut up and place in sauce pan with the water. Simmer, covered, 10 to 15 minutes until apples are soft. Add the honey and lemon juice and beat smooth with a whisk. Serve with dash of cinnamon or nutmeg.

Yield: about 1½ cups

Onion Sauce

1 cup milk
1 onion, sliced
¼ teaspoon salt
⅛ teaspoon mace
⅛ teaspoon pepper
2 tablespoons butter
2 tablespoons flour

Cook onion in milk with seasonings for 15 minutes. In another sauce pan, melt butter, stir in flour and cook 4-5 minutes. Add milk with onion, stir until thickened.

Yield: about 1½ cups

Brown Sauce

2 tablespoons butter
2 tablespoons flour
1 cup vegetable stock (page 32)
    or 1 teaspoon powdered vegetable bouillion
    dissolved in 1 cup hot water
Salt and pepper to taste

Brown the flour in a small dry skillet, stirring, but do not burn. Melt the butter, add the flour to form a roux, cook a few minutes. Add the vegetable stock, stirring with a whisk to blend well. Bring to a boil, simmer a few minutes. Add salt and pepper to taste.

Yield: 1 cup

Apricot Chutney

1 pound dried apricots
5 cups boiling water
10 cloves garlic
Fresh ginger root, 1" x 3" piece
1 onion, cut up
¼ cup cider vinegar
¼ teaspoon salt
½ teaspoon mustard seed
¼ teaspoon allspice
½ cup honey
¾ cup golden raisins
½ cup currants
½ cup walnuts, chopped

Pour boiling water over apricots and let stand overnight. Coarsely chop garlic and ginger root, place in blender with vinegar and onion. Blend. In heavy-bottomed pan, put apricots with soaking water and ground garlic, ginger mix. Add honey and spices. Simmer 45 minutes, covered, stirring occasionally, as mixture thickens. Add raisins, currant and walnuts and cook uncovered 30 to 40 minutes more. Mixture will be dark and thick; don't let it stick to the bottom of the pan. Pack into hot sterilized jars and seal.

Yield: 6 half-pint jars

Sweet Pepper Hash

12 large red sweet peppers
2 large Bermuda onions
1 ½ cups white vinegar
1 ½ cups sugar or 1 cup honey
1 ½ tablespoons salt

Remove seeds and membranes from peppers. Chop peppers and onions in processor. Pour boiling water over these and let stand for 5 minutes. Drain well. Bring vinegar, sugar and salt to a boil, add drained peppers and onions, cook for 15 minutes. Seal in sterile jars.

Yield: 6 half-pint jars

Hot Curried Fruit

1 17-ounce can peaches
1 17-ounce can mixed fruit or apricots
1 17-ounce can pineapple chunks
¼ cup butter
1 ½ teaspoons curry powder
¼ cup honey

Drain fruits well. Place in shallow buttered baking dish. Heat butter in skillet, add curry powder and cook a few minutes. Stir in the honey and cook about 5 minutes. Pour over the drained fruit. Bake uncovered at 350° about 35-40 minutes.

Grand Finales... *desserts*

Queen of Puddings

2 cups milk
2 ½ cups cake crumbs
2 tablespoons butter
¼ cup honey
2 eggs yolks (reserve whites for meringue)
Grated rind of 1 lemon
Raspberry jam

Heat milk in saucepan, adding butter, honey and cake crumbs. Cook gently for 2 minutes. Cool. Preheat oven. Beat the yolks lightly, stir in the milk mixture. Pour into a baking dish or 9″ pie plate and bake at 375° for 30 minutes. When cool, spread the top with jam and cover with meringue.

2 egg whites
¼ cup sugar
¼ teaspoon cream of tarter

Beat the whites, adding cream of tarter and adding the sugar gradually, until peaks form. Spread lightly on baked pudding. Bake at 300° for 15 minutes, until meringue is lightly browned.

Serves 6

Rice Pudding

2 cups cooked rice
1 ½ cups milk
3 tablespoons honey
1 tablespoon butter
1 teaspoon vanilla
2 eggs, lightly beaten
½ cup raisins
¼ teaspoon nutmeg

Heat the milk, adding honey, butter and vanilla. Raisins may be added to hot milk to plump up. Add milk and raisins to the eggs, then combine with the cooked rice. Put in buttered one-quart baking dish, sprinkle with nutmeg. Bake at 325° for 40 to 45 minutes.

Serve 6

Bread and Apple Pudding

4 slices whole wheat bread
1 cup milk
3 tablespoons honey
2 tablespoons butter
½ teaspoon cinnamon
½ teaspoon nutmeg
2 eggs, separated
1 ½ cups apples, peeled and cubed
½ cup raisins

Cut the bread into one-inch cubes. Heat the milk, adding honey, butter and spices. Pour hot milk over bread. Beat the egg yolks and stir into the bread and milk mixture. Add the apples and raisins. Beat the egg whites until stiff, then fold into the pudding. Pour into a buttered 1 ½ quart baking dish. Place dish in a pan of hot water. Bake at 350° 40-45 minutes. Good served warm or cold.

Serves 6

Cherry Custard Pudding

⅓ cup sugar
¼ cup cornstarch
3 eggs
2 cups scalded milk
1 tablespoon butter
1 ½ teaspoons vanilla
1 16-ounce can dark sweet cherries, pitted

Combine sugar and cornstarch. Beat eggs until lemon colored, add sugar and cornstarch and beat well. Pour in the scalded milk. Cook in a 2-quart saucepan over low heat until mixture thickens and starts to boil, stirring, about 10 minutes. Pour into serving dish to cool. Drain cherries, place cherries around top of pudding.

Serves 6

Caramel Custard

3 eggs
¾ cup sugar
2 cups milk, scalded
1 teaspoon vanilla

In a small, heavy skillet, heat one-half cup of sugar over medium low heat until the sugar melts and turns brown, stirring with a wooden spoon. Pour syrup into a one-quart bowl and rotate bowl to coat the sides. Preheat oven. Lightly beat the eggs, adding one-fourth cup sugar and vanilla. Whisk in the hot milk. Pour over the syrup in the bowl. Place custard dish in a pan of hot water and bake at 350° about 45 minutes. Custard is done when a knife inserted in center comes out clean. Remove from hot water and cool. To serve, run a knife around the edge and invert onto a round plate. This can be made in individual custard cups.

Serves 4

Chocolate Sponge Pudding

2 cups milk
2 squares unsweetened chocolate
¼ cup honey
3 eggs, separated
¼ cup flour
1 teaspoon vanilla

Heat the milk, melt the chocolate. Beat the egg yolks until light, adding the honey, flour and vanilla. Pour in the warm milk and chocolate, mix well. Beat the egg whites until soft peaks form, fold into the mixture. Pour into a buttered, round one-quart baking dish and place in pan of hot water. Preheat oven. Bake at 350° for 45-50 minutes. Serve with whipped cream, if desired.

Serves 4

Quick Coffee Mousse

½ pound marshmallows (30)
1 cup strong hot coffee
1 cup heavy cream
½ cup walnuts, chopped (optional)

Put hot coffee and marshmallows in top of double boiler, place over hot water and cook until marshmallows are dissolved, stirring occasionally. Chill. When this begins to set, whip the cream and fold in, adding nuts if desired. Pour into dessert dishes or a wet mold and chill until firm.

Serves 4

Apricot Mousse

4 ounces dried apricots (1 cup)
1 cup boiling water
¼ cup honey
2 eggs, separated
1 envelope plain gelatin (1 tablespoon)

Pour boiling water over apricots and let stand for 1 hour. Add honey, cover pan and cook over low heat 45 minutes to one hour, until apricots are soft. Cool for one hour. Place in blender or processor to puree apricots, adding the egg yolks. Soften the gelatin in ¼ cup cold water, add to apricots and yolks. Blend a few seconds. Place in top of double boiler over simmering water and cook for 10 minutes, stirring frequently. Cool for 30 minutes. Whip egg whites stiff, fold into apricots. Pour into serving glasses or a wet mold and chill.

Serves 6

Chocolate Mousse

4 eggs, separated
¾ cup sugar
1 tablespoon instant coffee
¼ cup hot water
½ cup butter, room temperature
6 ounces semi-sweet chocolate
¼ cup orange juice
¼ teaspoon cream of tarter

Dissolve the instant coffee in the hot water, then add sugar and cook over low heat until sugar is dissolved. Beat the egg yolks for 2 minutes until thickened. Beat in the coffee mixture slowly. Place mixture in top of double boiler over simmering water. Beat, while cooking, for 5 or 6 minutes. Remove from heat, continue beating for about 5 minutes until foamy and cooled. Melt the chocolate in the orange juice, over low heat. Stir in the butter. Cool slightly, then add to egg yolks. Beat the egg whites with the cream of tarter until the whites form soft peaks. Gently fold the whites, using a spatula or rubber scraper, into the chocolate and egg mixture. Turn into a serving dish or individual molds. Chill.

Serves 6

Chocolate Charlotte

1 dozen lady-fingers
1 recipe chocolate mousse (page 113)

Place a circle of waxed paper in the bottom of a straight sided 5 cup mold. Split lady fingers in half lengthwise. (Thin slices of pound cake can be substituted.) Line the bottom and sides of the mold with lady fingers, pour in the mousse mixture. Top with remaining lady fingers. Chill. Invert onto a plate to serve. This can be frozen, but remove from refrigerator 15 minutes before serving to make slicing easier. Serve with whipped cream if desired.

Serves 6

Chocolate Souffle

¼ cup butter
2 ounces (2 squares) unsweetened chocolate
¼ cup flour
1 cup milk
3 eggs, separated
½ cup sugar
¼ teaspoon mace
1 teaspoon vanilla

Melt the butter and chocolate in the top of a double boiler. Add the flour, stirring to blend. Add the milk, stirring constantly and cook until it forms a very thick sauce. Set aside to cool. Beat the egg yolks until light and lemon colored, add the sugar and beat well. Add mace and vanilla. Stir the sauce into the egg yolks, blending thoroughly. Preheat oven. Beat the egg whites until soft peaks form, then gently fold whites into the sauce mixture. Butter a 1 ½ quart round baking dish and sprinkle sugar on the bottom. Pour in the souffle mix. Place dish in a pan of hot water 1 inch deep. Bake at 325° for 1 hour, serve at once.

Serves 6

Orange Souffle

¼ cup butter
6 tablespoons flour
1 cup milk
3 eggs, separated
½ sugar
3 tablespoons orange juice
1 tablespoon grated orange rind
1 tablespoon lemon juice

Melt the butter in a heavy bottomed saucepan. Add the flour and stir to blend. Add the milk and cook until sauce is very thick. Cool. Beat the egg yolks until light and lemon colored, add the sugar and beat well. Add the orange juice and peel and the lemon juice. Stir the sauce mixture into the egg yolks. Preheat oven. Beat the egg whites until soft peaks form, fold carefully into sauce. Butter a 1½ quart baking dish and sprinkle sugar on the bottom. Pour in souffle mixture. Place in a pan of hot water 1 inch deep. bake at 325° for 1 hour. Serve hot.

Serves 6

Meringue Shells

3 egg whites
1 cup sugar
¼ teaspoon cream of tarter
½ teaspoon baking powder
1 teaspoon vanilla
1 teaspoon vinegar
1 teaspoon water

Sift together the sugar, cream of tarter and baking powder. Mix vanilla, vinegar and water in a small bowl. Beat the egg whites until soft peaks form, then slowly add the sifted sugar, starting with a teaspoonful, as you beat. When half the sugar is added, alternate sugar with a teaspoon of the liquid. Beat whites until sugar is dissolved. Place brown paper on a cookie sheet. Spoon meringues into six rounds on the paper. Bake in a slow oven, 250° for one hour. Remove from paper and keep in an airtight tin to preserve crispness. Serve filled with fresh fruit or ice cream and sauce.

Serves 6

Forgotten Cookies

1 recipe for meringue shells
1 6-ounce package chocolate chips

Follow directions for meringue shells. After sugar is beaten into whites, fold in the chocolate chips. Preheat oven to 300°. Drop mix by teaspoonsful on lightly buttered cookie sheet. Turn off heat, put cookies in oven and leave in overnight. Do not open oven door to peek.

Yield: 48 cookies

Lemon Filled Shells

6 baked meringue shells (see facing page)
3 egg yolks, beaten
½ cup sugar
1 tablespoon flour
½ cup water
1 cup heavy cream
Juice and grated rind of 1 lemon

Dissolve flour and sugar in water, add beaten yolks, lemon rind and juice. Cook in the top of a double boiler over simmering water, stirring, until the filling is thick. Whip the cream. Into each shell place a layer of whipped cream, then a later of lemon filling, then a top layer of cream. Chill overnight or several hours.

Serves 6

Pecan Tarts

½ cup butter
3 ounces cream cheese
1 cup flour

Mix these ingredients for the dough and press into the bottoms and sides of 24 small (1¾″) muffin tins.

Filling:

1 cup pecans, finely chopped
1 egg
¾ cup brown sugar
1 tablespoon melted butter
½ teaspoon vanilla

Mix filling ingredients together and spoon into muffin cups. Preheat oven. Bake at 375° for 20 to 25 minutes.

Yield: 24 tarts

Peach Cream Pie

One unbaked pie shell (page 119)
3 large fresh peaches
¾ cup sugar
2 tablespoons flour
1 cup heavy cream or half and half

Peel the peaches, cut each in half and place cut side up in the unbaked shell. Sprinkle with ¼ cup of the sugar. Mix remaining ½ cup of sugar with the flour and stir into the cream. Pour over the peaches. Preheat oven. Bake at 400° for 50 minutes.

Serves 6

Rhubarb Cream Pie

Pastry for double-crust 9″ pie (this page)
3 cups fresh rhubarb, cut in 1″ pieces
1 ½ cups sugar
3 tablespoons flour
½ teaspoon nutmeg
1 tablespoon melted butter
2 eggs, lightly beaten

Line pie pan with half the pastry. Put rhubarb in. Mix sugar, four and nutmeg, add the butter and eggs. Pour batter over rhubarb. Top with crust, crimp edges and slash (top) crust in several places. Preheat oven. Bake for 10 minutes at 450°, then reduce heat to 350° and bake 30 minutes more.

Serves 6

Pastry Crust

2 cups flour
½ teaspoon salt
½ cup butter, very cold
2 tablespoons vegetable shortening
4 to 6 tablespoons cold water

Cut cold butter into 8 or 9 pieces. With processor or a pastry blender, combine flour, salt, butter and shortening. Sprinkle with very cold water until mixture can be pressed into a ball. Divide into two balls and chill. This will make 2 9″ pie shells or one double-crust pie. Roll crusts into a circle on a lightly floured surface, fit into pie plate and press edges with a fork or flute between thumb and finger. For a baked shell, preheat oven, prick crust on bottom and sides with a fork, then bake at 375° 20 minutes until golden brown.

Lemon Meringue Pie

One baked 9 inch pie shell (see pastry, page 119)
1 cup sugar
2 tablespoons cornstarch
¼ cup flour
¼ teaspoon salt
2 cups boiling water
1 ½ teaspoons grated lemon rind
6 tablespoons lemon juice (2 lemons)
2 tablespoons butter
3 eggs, separated
6 tablespoons sugar for meringue

Combine sugar, cornstarch, flour and salt. Gradually add the 2 cups of boiling water and cook 10 minutes, stirring constantly as mixture thickens. Lightly beat the 3 egg yolks, add the lemon rind and juice. Add a little hot sauce to the yolks, then combine with remaining sauce. Cook this mixture 2 minutes, stirring. Cool slightly, then turn into the prebaked pastry shell. Whip the egg whites until stiff, slowly adding the 6 tablespoons of sugar. Spread meringue on top of lemon filling. Preheat oven. Bake at 350° for about 15 minutes until meringue browns slightly.

Serves 6

Lemon Cheese Pie

Graham Cracker Crust

1 ½ cups graham cracker crumbs
½ cup sugar
¼ cup melted butter

In an 8 or 9 inch pie plate, mix the crumbs with the butter and sugar with a fork and press firmly onto the bottom and sides of the pan.

Filling

8 ounces cream cheese, at room temperature
2 tablespoons melted butter
¾ cup sugar
2 eggs
⅔ cups milk
2 tablespoons flour
Juice and grated rind of 2 lemons

Combine cream cheese, butter, sugar, eggs, milk, flour and the juice and grated lemon rind. Blend or process until smooth and creamy. Pour mixture into pie crust. Top may be sprinkled with graham cracker crumbs. Preheat oven. Bake at 350° for 30 to 40 minutes. Cool. Serve chilled.

Serves 8

Lemon Ice

2 cups water
1 cup sugar
Grated rind of 1 lemon
Juice of 2 lemons

Combine sugar, water and lemon rind and bring to a boil. Cook for 5 minutes, cool. Add the lemon juice. Freeze until firm. Remove from freezer 10 minutes before serving to soften.

Yield: 1 pint

Orange Ice

2 cups water
1 cup sugar
Grated rind of 1 orange
1 cup orange juice
2 tablespoons lemon juice

Combine sugar and water and bring to a boil, cook 5 minutes. Add the grated rind, orange juice and lemon juice. Strain, then freeze until firm. Remove from freezer 10 minutes before serving to soften.

Yield: 3 cups

Raspberry Fool

2 cups fresh raspberries (or strawberries)
honey or sugar to taste
1 cup heavy cream, whipped or 1 cup sour cream

Puree one cup of the fruit in the blender, adding honey to taste. Whip the cream. Fold the puree and the remaining cup of whole berries into the cream. Chill several hours. Serve in glass dishes with cookies.

Serve 4

Pineapple Snow

1 envelope plain gelatin (1 tablespoon)
¼ cup water
1 can crushed pineapple (1lb. 4 oz.)
1 cup heavy cream, whipped

Soften gelatin in the cold water. Heat the pineapple with its juice. If unsweetened, add 2 tablespoons honey or sweeten to taste. When pineapple is boiling, stir in the gelatin to dissolve. Allow to cool, then chill until nearly firm. Whip the cream and fold into the pineapple, pour into serving dishes or a wet mold. Chill.

Serves 6

Vanilla Ice Cream

2 cups milk or half and half
¼ cup honey
1 large egg
1 teaspoon vanilla

Heat one cup of milk, adding the honey. Beat the egg, add the hot milk and cook over low heat until mixture is a thin custard. Remove from heat, add the other cup of milk and the vanilla. Place in freezer until firm. Remove about 10 minutes before serving to soften.

Serves 4

Chocolate Ice Cream

Vanilla ice cream recipe
2 ounces semi-sweet chocolate

Melt the chocolate and add to the hot milk in the vanilla ice cream recipe.

Strawberry Ice Cream

1 recipe vanilla ice cream
1½ cups strawberries (or 1 10-ounce package frozen)
honey if berries are unsweetened

Cut up the berries, adding honey to taste if unsweetened. Fold into the vanilla ice cream after it has been in the freezer about 30 minutes. Peaches may also be used.

Pears Helene

3 firm pears
⅔ cup sugar
2 cups water
1 teaspoon vanilla
Chocolate Fudge Sauce (page 126)
Vanilla Ice Cream

Peel the pears, cut in half lengthwise and remove cores. Combine the sugar and water and bring to a boil. Add the pears, cover the pan and cook over low heat about 5 minutes, turning pears once. Pears should be tender. Add vanilla to syrup and let pears cool. Place each pear half on a scoop of ice cream, rounded side up, and top with chocolate fudge sauce.

   Canned pear halves can be used. Add 1 teaspoon of vanilla to the syrup in the can and let pears sit for several hours, then drain.

Serves 6

Butterscotch Sauce

3 tablespoons butter
¼ cup corn syrup
½ cup brown sugar

Melt butter, add syrup and sugar. Bring to a boil and cook 1 minute, stirring. If too thick after standing, stir in a tablespoon of boiling water, or reheat.

Yield: ½ cup

Chocolate Fudge Sauce

1 square unsweetened chocolate
¼ cup sugar
2 tablespoons corn syrup
2 tablespoons milk
1 tablespoon butter
½ teaspoon vanilla

Place all ingredients except vanilla in heavy bottomed saucepan and cook until sugar is dissolved, stirring. Boil mixture about 5 minutes, stirring occasionally. Remove from heat, beat in vanilla. Can be served hot or cold.

Yield: ½ cup

Red Currant Sauce

¼ cup red currant jelly
1 cup hot water
1 teaspoon cornstarch
1 teaspoon lemon juice

Heat the jelly and water. Dissolve cornstarch in the lemon juice, add to the jelly. Bring to a boil and cook 2 to 3 minutes until thickened.

Yield: 1 cup

Peach Melba

1 pint vanilla ice cream
2 large peaches
1 cup red currant sauce

Peel and slice the peaches, arrange slices around servings of the ice cream and top with cool red currant sauce.

Serves 4

Blueberry Crumble

¼ cup butter, softened
¾ cup sugar
1 egg
½ cup milk
2 cups flour
2 teaspoons baking powder
½ teaspoon salt
2 cups blueberries

Butter a 9″ x 9″ pan. Mix the butter, sugar, egg and milk together. Stir in the flour, baking powder and salt. Stir to blend, then add blueberries. Put into baking dish. Preheat oven. Mix topping:

½ cup sugar
⅓ cup flour
½ teaspoon cinnamon
¼ cup butter, softened

Sprinkle topping over batter. bake at 375° for 45 minutes. Delicious served warm.

Serves 8

Cranberry Crisp

1 cup rolled oats
½ cup flour
¼ teaspoon salt
1 cup brown sugar
1 teaspoon grated orange rind
⅓ cup butter, softened
2 cups cranberry sauce (page 100)

Mix together the oats, flour, salt, sugar and orange peel. Add butter and mix until crumbly. Pat half the mixture into a buttered 9″ x 9″ pan. Cover with cranberry sauce. Top with remaining crumbs. Preheat oven. Bake at 350° 40 to 45 minutes. Cut in squares and serve warm with vanilla ice cream.

Serves 8

Apple Crisp: Use 2 cups applesauce (page 104) instead of cranberry sauce.

Peach Cobbler

6-7 peaches
2 tablespoons butter
¼ to ½ cup sugar

Peel and slice the peaches into a buttered 8″ x 8″ baking dish. Sprinkle with sugar and dot with butter.

Prepare batter:
2 eggs
2 tablespoons water
½ cup sugar
½ cup flour
½ teaspoon baking powder
dash of nutmeg

Beat the eggs with the water, add sugar, flour. baking powder and nutmeg. Mix well, pour over peaches. Preheat oven. Bake at 350° for 30 minutes. Serve warm.

Serves 6

Baked Bananas

4 bananas
1 orange, juice and rind
1 tablespoon honey

Slice bananas lengthwise and place halves in buttered pie plate. Grate orange rind and squeeze ½ cup of juice. Add 1 teaspoon grated rind and the juice to the honey and pour over bananas. Preheat oven. Bake at 350° 30 minutes. Serve hot.

Serves 4

Baked Apples

4 large apples
½ cup almonds or pecans, chopped
2 tablespoons melted butter
2 tablespoons honey
Cinnamon (optional)

Core apples and place in buttered baking dish. Stuff cavities with nuts. Melt butter and honey, pour into cavities. Preheat oven. Bake 30 to 40 minutes at 375° until apples are tender. Sprinkle with cinnamon if desired.

Serves 4

Walnut Oblongs

¾ cup butter
½ cup sugar
1 cup flour
⅔ cup walnuts, finely chopped
1 teaspoon vanilla
½ cup chocolate chips

Mix ingredients in processor or with slotted spoon. Shape dough into a rectangle one-half inch thick between two sheets of waxed paper. Chill for one hour. Mark into 48 pieces. As each piece is broken off, shape it into an oblong shape and place on a lightly greased baking sheet. These will melt down while cooking so leave space between cookies. Preheat oven. Bake at 350° about 10-12 minutes. Remove from baking sheet and cool. Melt ½ cup chocolate chips in a small bowl, dip one end of each cookie into the chocolate. Cool.

Yield: 48 cookies

Chocolate Shortbread Cookies

½ pound butter
½ cup confectioners sugar
1½ cups flour
⅜ cup cornstarch
3 tablespoons cocoa

Cream the butter and sugar, gradually add flour, cornstarch and cocoa. Blend well. Turn dough out onto a floured surface. Roll out or pat down to ¼ inch thickness. Cut in small rounds. Prick each twice with a fork. Put on lightly buttered baking sheet and chill for 30 minutes. Preheat oven to 375° and bake for 5 minutes. Reduce heat to 300° and bake 12 to 15 minutes more.

Yield: 36 cookies

Oatmeal Raisin Cookies

1 ½ cups flour
½ teaspoon baking powder
1 teaspoon cinnamon
½ teaspoon nutmeg
½ cup honey (or 1 cup sugar)
½ cup melted butter
½ cup melted vegetable shortening
1 tablespoon molasses
1 egg
1 ¾ cup rolled oats
1 teaspoon vanilla
1 cup raisins
2 tablespoons to ¼ cup boiling water

Pour the boiling water over the raisins to plump them, using only 2 tablespoons if honey is used, or ¼ cup if sugar is used. Combine all the other ingredients except oatmeal and stir. Add the oatmeal and raisins. Preheat oven to 350°. Drop cookie dough by teaspoonfuls on ungreased cookie sheets and bake 10 minutes.

Yield: 60 cookies

Pecan Balls

½ cup butter
2 tablespoons honey
1 teaspoon vanilla
1 cup flour
½ teaspoon salt
1 cup pecans, finely chopped

Cream the butter, honey and vanilla until fluffy. Add the flour and salt, blending thoroughly. Add the chopped nuts and mix well. Shape unto balls the size of walnuts, place on a greased baking sheet. Bake at 325° about 20 minutes. Cool slightly, then roll in confectioner's sugar.

Yield: 30

Desserts / 133

Apple Torte

2 eggs
1 cup sugar
¼ cup flour
2 ½ teaspoons baking powder
2 large apples, peeled and chopped
½ cup chopped walnuts
1 teaspoon vanilla

Beat the eggs well, add sugar and beat. Beat in the flour and baking powder. Stir in the apples, nuts and vanilla. Pour into a buttered 9″ x 9″ baking dish. Preheat oven. Bake at 325° for 40 minutes, cut into squares while warm. This will puff up and then settle down on cooling. Good served warm or cold.

Serves 6

Trifle

4 cups leftover cake (white, yellow, lemon or a 13-ounce frozen pound cake)
1 3½ ounce package vanilla pudding
1 10-ounce package frozen raspberries or strawberries, thawed
1 cup heavy cream, whipped

Cut cake into one-inch cubes. Prepare pudding according to package directions. In a glass serving bowl, alternate layers of cake, fruit and pudding, then top with whipped cream. Chill several hours or overnight to let fruit juices soak into cake. If fresh fruit is used, sweeten to taste.

Serves 6

Walnut Meringue Cake

4 eggs, separated
1⅔ cup sugar
1 cup sifted flour
1½ teaspoons baking powder
½ teaspoon lemon extract
¼ teaspoon salt
5 tablespoons boiling water
¼ teaspoon cream of tarter
¾ cup chopped walnuts
¾ cup crushed pineapple, well drained
1 cup heavy cream, whipped

Cut circles of waxed paper for bottoms of two 8 inch layer cake pans. Butter the pan and the paper. Beat the egg yolks, gradually add ⅔ cup of sugar, the salt and lemon extract. Beat well. Add the flour and baking powder and beat. Spread this batter evenly in the two cake pans. Make a meringue by beating the egg whites stiffly, adding the cream of tarter and 1 cup sugar. Preheat oven. Spread the meringue on top of the batter and sprinkle with the chopped nuts. Bake at 350° for 35-40 minutes. Cool on a rack. Put one layer on a cake plate, nut side down. Whip the cream and fold in the drained crushed pineapple. Spread on the bottom cake layer. Place other cake on top of filling with the meringue and nut side up. Chill. This can be made the day before.

Serves 8

Fruit Cake

Prepare 3 loaf pans (9" x 5" x 3") by greasing well with vegetable shortening, then line with foil, cut to overhang the sides. Press out wrinkles, then grease the foil.

4 eggs
1 ¾ cups brown sugar, firmly packed
¾ cup butter, softened
½ cup molasses
1 cup orange juice
8 ounces dates (1 ¼ cups), cut up
1 pound chopped candied fruit
1 pound raisins
¼ pound candied cherries
¼ pound candied pineapple
2 cups pecans or walnuts, broken in pieces
3 cups flour
2 teaspoons baking powder
1 teaspoon salt
2 teaspoons cinnamon
½ teaspoon allspice
½ teaspoon ground cloves
½ teaspoon nutmeg

Sift the flour, spices, baking powder and salt together and mix some with the cut up fruit. Beat the eggs until foamy, add the brown sugar and the butter and beat well. Add the molasses and half the orange juice. Stir in half the flour, mix well, then add remaining juice. Stir, then add remaining flour and the fruits and nuts. Combine and divide mixture into the 3 prepared loaf pans. Bake at 275° for two hours, or until cake is done. Cool for 30 minutes before removing from pans, then lift up foil and remove foil. Wrapped well, this will keep for 3 to 4 weeks in the refrigerator, or several months in the freezer.

Makes 3 fruit cakes.

Sample Menus for a 4 or 5 Course Dinner

Stuffed Mushrooms (p. 26.)
Leek Soup (p. 38)
Walnut Cheese Balls (p. 86)   Glazed Butternut Squash (p. 84)
Potato-Tomato-Mushroom Scallop (p. 69)
Garbanzo Bean Salad (p. 47)
Apple Torte (p. 134)

Chutney Cheese Squares (p. 24)
Cold Cucumber Soup (p. 36)
Mushroom Tarts (p. 67)   Spinach Souffle (p. 77)
Cream Cheese and Fruit Salad (p. 49)
Coffee Mousse (p. 112)   Walnut Oblongs (p. 132)

Tomatoes Bengal (p. 27)
Potato Soup (p. 36)   Devilled Crackers (p. 40)
Linguine with Mushrooms (p. 62)
Stuffed Zucchini (p. 81) Salad Greens with Herb Dressing (p. 54)
Lemon Cheese Pie (p. 121)

Cheese Olive Balls (p. 24)
Tomato Consomme (p. 39)
Lentil and Rice Roast (p. 88)   with Brown Sauce (p. 104)
Corn Pudding (p. 59)   Hot Curried Fruit (p. 106)
Spinach and Mushroom Salad (p. 42)
Caramel Custard (p. 110)

Onion Cheese Puffs (p. 25)
Creamy Vegetable Soup (p. 38)
Cabbage Pie (p. 59)   Millet and Peas (p. 64)
Avocado and Orange Salad (p. 45)   with French Dressing (p. 53)
Chocolate Mousse (p. 113)   or Chocolate Sponge Pudding (p. 111)

Olive Stuffed Eggs (p. 24)
Cheese Soup (p. 39)   Herb Toast (p. 40)
Nut Cutlets (p. 96)   with Bernaise Sauce (p. 101)
New Potatoes and Peas with Dill (p. 94)
Garbanzo Bean Salad (p. 47)
Trifle with Strawberries (p. 134)

Cucumber Canapes (p. 25)
Lentil Soup (p. 34)   Cheese Twists (p. 26)
Curried Vegetables on Rice (p. 61)   Apricot Chutney (p. 105)
Brussel Sprouts with Almonds (p. 87)
Tomato Aspic Salad (p. 52)   with Mayonnaise (p. 54)
Walnut Meringue Cake (p. 135)

Armenian Beans (p. 27)
Tomato Soup (p. 37)   with Croutons (p. 40)
Nut and Rice Roast (p. 96)   with Cumberland Sauce (p. 100)
Baked Onions (p. 83)   Savory Eggplant (p. 73)
Cucumber and Dill Salad (p. 43)
Peach Cobbler (p. 129)

Index